You and the
MASS MEDIA

August Franza

J. WESTON
WALCH
PUBLISHER

Portland, Maine

About the Author

August Franza has a Ph.D. in English and has taught in public schools and colleges for 40 years. As early as the 1960's, he pioneered programs in communications and the mass media. He has written extensively on the subject, having published more than 100 articles that reflect his concern about the influence of the media. He has spoken at conferences and appeared on local talk shows as he worked to inform teachers and students about their responsibilities as civic-minded media watchers.

1 2 3 4 5 6 7 8 9 10

ISBN 0-8251-3773-X

Copyright © 1989, 1998
J. Weston Walch, Publisher
P. O. Box 658 • Portland, Maine 04104-0658

Printed in the United States of America

Contents

To the Student   iv

To the Teacher   v

Assessing Student Performance   vii

PAGE

1	CHAPTER 1.	The World of Media
12	CHAPTER 2.	Television: Is This Your Life?
32	CHAPTER 3.	Radio: The Intimate Medium
45	CHAPTER 4.	Film: The Big Picture
60	CHAPTER 5.	Journalism: The Great Debate
73	CHAPTER 6.	Propaganda: The Worm in the Apple
88	CHAPTER 7.	Advertising: The Big Pitch
105	CHAPTER 8.	Censorship

To the Student

Welcome to an investigation of your role in the mass media. This text is designed to make you aware of the powerful media that influence your life. It is also designed to help you develop a critical attitude. In order to have a set of personal standards, you have to examine what you're thinking. To that end, many of the exercises in this book are designed to help you discover what you know, what you like and dislike, what your opinions are—in effect, where you stand at this point in your life on some very important issues.

Each mass medium is given its own chapter. There are also chapters on propaganda, advertising, and censorship. When you complete this book, you should be better informed, much more alert to the media you use every day, and better able to make judgments and decisions about the mass media, which are always trying to influence you.

To the Teacher

This book of activities has been written to invite students to examine, think about, and respond to the mass media. It has been designed so that students will employ all of the important basic and more-sophisticated skills they have been learning through their school years: reading, writing, researching, discussing, thinking, interpreting, debating.

Since I encourage students to state their raw opinions often, let me say a word or two about that practice. Thirty years of public school teaching (along with years of college and senior citizen teaching) have taught me that the best way for students to improve all of their skills, as well as their self-esteem, is to encourage use of these skills, no matter how elementary or undeveloped they seem to the teacher.

It's obvious that most students have very little hard information about the mass media, and they've probably read or thought little on the subject. Why, then, do I ask them to pass judgment so often? Because I want to welcome them into the fray! I do not agree with the viewpoint that says, "You cannot discuss this matter or have an opinion until you have matured, or until you have read or thought long enough to have considered, well-documented views." Under this line of reasoning, many people will never be ready to state opinions, get involved in a subject enough to care about it, and hear and read different points of view. Meanwhile, the media continue to have their effects whether or not students (who are also citizens) are examining what they are experiencing daily. It therefore seems reasonable to me to welcome all students into the debate about the mass media, whatever their experience, expertise, and ability, and to welcome them with enthusiasm, openness, and encouragement. The goal, of course, is to become well-informed.

Having said all of the above, I do not wish to suggest that there is nothing substantial about what is to follow. There is, on the contrary, a great deal of substance in *You and the Mass Media*, and it makes many demands on students. When they have completed all of the activities and exercises, this book will be filled with fascinating and provocative information, observations, questions, and imaginings. Students should be able to look at the media, at their language, and even at themselves with a new alertness and awareness.

I wish to stress the importance of library use for the full success of *You and the Mass Media*. Every library—school, public, or private—is a powerhouse of information that many students fail to employ satisfactorily. Maybe it's because the library is not a place for socializing. Maybe it's because adolescents feel intimidated by the avalanche of information in a library. Maybe it's because there's a psychic conflict between their emergence as individuals and their need to be helped to use the mass of information that sits inertly on the shelves. Whatever the reasons, I know that most students underuse a library, and we've got to encourage and persuade them to do the opposite! As a result of these considerations, many activities in *You and the Mass Media* require use of the library.

You should know that *You and the Mass Media* is designed to meet national social studies standards as established by the National Council for the Social Studies. As you know, the primary purpose of social studies is to help young people develop the ability to make informed and reasoned decisions for the public good as citizens of a culturally diverse, democratic society in an interdependent world. Another purpose is to manage technology so that the greatest number of people benefit from it. Since the mass media are the major way citizens get their information, it is necessary that they examine these media and recognize the impact on their lives. Civic competence in our society, an important goal of social studies, is influenced very strongly by the media. Some critics think that the media create consumers rather than civic activists and that this is not helpful in creating students able to assume "the office of citizen" (as Thomas Jefferson called it). Furthermore, the national social studies standards invite activities that address "the contemporary conditions of real life and of academic scholarship." *You and the Mass Media* meets these goals by helping students construct a personal perspective as well as an academic one. Students will gather information, reflect, and learn to read, write, and think critically.

Assessing Student Performance

While many of the activities in *You and the Mass Media* are open-ended and subjective, there are concrete ways of assessing student performance. These are:

1. extended written assignments
2. oral reports
3. projects
4. tests and quizzes on the contents of chapters, key vocabulary words, and definitions of terms
5. keeping a journal

1. Written assignments   There is no better way to assess students' performance and progress than to ask them to produce a coherent essay on a pertinent topic. Observing how students organize their thoughts, use details, and analyze the results of their research will tell you a great deal about how well they are absorbing and applying the content of each chapter. As you will note, there are many writing assignments in the text. The evaluation of student writing must be a key factor in determining grades.

2. Oral reports   Listening to students explain their encounters with the media—reporting what they see and hear—is another concrete means of assessment. For example, students may watch no TV at all for one week and report their reactions to the class in terms of what they did with their time, what they thought they were missing, what their reactions were. Did they feel out of touch? Did they have a positive experience? Were they bored? Were they unable to occupy themselves usefully?

3. Projects   Students are assigned the creation of their own short movies, tapes, collages, ads, and interviews of local people working in the media. Then they present their work to the class.

4. Tests and quizzes   You could ask students to define mass media, television, prime time, and the terms in each chapter. Who wrote the original *War of the Worlds*? Who wrote the radio version? etc. There are scores of significant specific facts in *You and the Mass Media* that students must make a part of their media vocabulary and consciousness.

A Definition

Mass Media are those means of communication (TV, movies, CDs, tapes, the Internet, newspapers, books, and magazines) that reach and influence millions of people.

vii

5. Journal Granted, journals are subjective, but students need discipline to keep them. Requirements for journals can be simple but clear-cut. Entries should be about the media, with reactions to all aspects: television, advertising, movies, magazines and newspapers, radio, the Internet. There should be a certain number of pages required each month. The journal must be legible. All entries must be dated.

CHAPTER 1

The World of Media

The word *media* means "ways of transmission." It's the Latin plural of *medium*. When we put the word *mass* in front of *media*, we mean ways of transmission to very large audiences in the tens of millions and beyond.

What exactly is being transmitted, and how does it reach so many people at once? Let's start by looking at the most basic aspects of mass media.

The world of media is made up of pictures, words, and sound. To make progress in trying to understand all three of these ingredients of media, let's think a moment about each of the three factors.

1. Pictures, of course, are the most powerful component of media. The old cliché that "a picture is worth a thousand words" is, in many ways, absolutely true. (But not in *all* ways; we'll come back to this thought later on.)

    When you are shown a house on a television or movie screen, you know what it is immediately. You also know immediately whether it is an old house, a new house, an attractive house, or a run-down house. You see a great many of the details of the house all at once, whereas in print you would have to read a page of print, line by line, to learn about these details.

    The print experience is slower, whereas the picture experience is faster. Here, also, the pictures reflect your daily visual experience, so you are attracted to the TV or movie screen because of the familiarity.

2. Words are the only part of the media that do not have a counterpart in life, except as sounds. Words, as such, do not exist as pictures and sounds do. They are completely the invention of the human mind. Nevertheless, the media must use words because we hear them and read them in life. Without words there would be an enormous loss of information and ideas.

You'll recall that I said that the cliché "a picture is worth a thousand words" is true in many ways but not in *all* ways. Suppose that behind the house in your picture there is a deep ravine that is not visible. Or suppose there is a garbage dump right next to the house but it's not shown. Words are then needed to complete the truth of the situation.

When we talk about ideas like democracy or freedom or good health, we have no pictures, and therefore we need words. Words are the only medium that can explain these ideas or concepts. Even a picture, as informative as it is, has its limitations. These limitations can be minimized by words. Once again, words are necessary in the media because there are ideas to communicate, and words do that job best.

3. Because sounds exist in the world they must be placed in the media. When we hear them in the media, we say to ourselves automatically, "Oh, yes, those sounds are the same ones I hear in my daily life: a whistle, a plane, a conversation, a piece of music."

Sound is necessary to complete the picture of reality that the media must show us if we are to take an interest in them. No one would watch *Seinfeld*, *Dallas* or *Monday Night Football* if there were no sound. Before 1930, when there was no sound in the movies, each theater had a piano and a piano-player who accompanied the action on the screen with live music. For the broadcast media to do their job, which is to attract an audience, they must include sound.

Pictures. Words. Sound. These are the ingredients of the media. Used in proper combinations, they have a mighty attraction for us. We know this is true because of the popularity of TV, movies, magazines, newspapers, radio, records, tapes, and, of course, books.

In order to fully understand the power of pictures, sounds, and words in our lives, try doing some sensory deprivation experiments.

1. Listen to TV for a half hour with a blindfold on your eyes. Describe here your feelings and reactions:

   _____

   _____

   _____

2. Watch TV with the sound off for a half-hour. Describe here your feelings and reactions.

   _____

   _____

   _____

3. In your English class, spend a period wearing a blindfold and earplugs so that you cannot read or hear words. Describe your reactions and feelings.

_____
_____
_____

4. Which was the worse form of deprivation, not to hear or not to see? Explain your choice.

_____
_____
_____

The term "mass media" means that the same pictures, words, and sounds are being seen and heard by anywhere from 20 million to 80 million people. (A Super Bowl game is seen by 140 million people, for example.) This is something to think about.

Think what it means to a manufacturer of a new product, a president with a message, or an association of doctors who want to inform a large number of people about a new finding. Think what it means to a news company that has to report the news it's collected over the past 24 hours. Think what it means to a man or woman who wants to attract attention to a cause. Think what it means to a movie producer who has a handsome new star to show the public. And think what it means to a person or group who wants to communicate to the mass audience, but can't. How does that person feel?

There has been nothing in human history equal to the power of the media in the 20th century. Even if a book sells 100,000 copies, does that number compare to the tens of millions of people who *daily* watch TV and movies? It's been said that in one night of television, more people will see a production of a Shakespeare play than the total number of those who have seen it in the theater since Shakespeare's time. And he died in 1616.

What are your personal reactions to these realities, facts, and statistics? Using the space on the following page, write a commentary called "Living With the Mass Media," or "The Mass Media in My House," or "Life Without the Mass Media." Include your thoughts, observations, feelings, and questions as they occur to you. Jot down whatever comes to mind at first, then organize it. Do this for homework and share it with your class.

It is important to write down your thoughts, because it helps you remember what you have learned and often reveals thoughts and opinions you didn't know you had.

Title _____

_____

- **After you complete the exercise,** let's continue our discussion of the media. Because of the numbers of people involved, there are consequences of mass media. Turn your attention to four of these consequences: personal, economic, artistic, and political. Let's take them one at a time.

1. **Personal:** With so many media available to you, you have decisions to make. After all, you don't have endless amounts of time to spend watching and using the media. You've got school, homework, chores, and maybe a job. We know from many studies that the mass media absorb a great deal of our time. Television apparently absorbs most of it. The average American family has the TV set on for at least seven and a quarter hours a day. The radio occupies some of your time, so does your stereo, and so do videotapes.

   So consciously or not, we commit small and large amounts of time to the media. Studies have shown that Americans spend *more time watching TV than*

any other activity except work and sleep. Write down your reaction to this fact. Do you think it's good, bad, wise, or foolish?

_____

_____

Try an experiment. Examine your own media behavior for a week by keeping a log of the media you use and the amount of time you spend using them. Using the chart, keep a record of every time you watch TV, listen to the radio, play your stereo, see a movie, etc. Indicate the date, identify the activity, and the amount of time spent. Do this for one week. And don't cheat! Report your conclusions to the class.

Date	Activity (Be specific; name stations and shows.)	Time Spent

> • **After you complete the chart,** report your week's behaviors to the class. Evaluate them. Are you satisfied with the amount of time you spend using the media? Are you surprised? Are you dissatisfied? Do you want to change your behavior?

_____
_____
_____
_____
_____
_____
_____

2. **Economic:** There are great amounts of money involved in the mass media. Some of it is yours.

   In the United States, the media are privately owned. A company like CBS leases the airwaves from the public through the Federal Communications Commission. As long as it can prove that it serves the public in doing so, it can organize programming and sell TV time to companies that want to advertise their products to you.

   This airtime gets very expensive when millions of people will be watching any particular commercial. CBS, for example, can charge a great deal of money for each minute of commercial time during the Super Bowl because 140 million viewers may hear a company's message. The amount of money a TV station demands depends on the size of the audience. (How the size of the audience is determined will be discussed later.) The company is willing to pay $2,000,000 or more per minute of advertising time because it knows that even if only one percent of the audience actually buys the product, the company gets 2,800,000 sales. If the product costs two dollars, the advertiser's income is $5,600,000. As they say, "It pays to advertise."

   As part of this purchasing public, you often have to decide how much of what appeals to you in TV advertising you can actually afford. Furthermore, how do you know which products are good ones and which are poor ones? You have to ask yourself questions about how the commercial makers employ their skill to make you want to spend your money on their products.

   Name some products you have used that are as good as they are advertised to be:

_____
_____

Name some products you have used that are *not* as good as they are advertised to be:

_____

_____

3. **Artistic:** One artistic consequence is very positive. TV is a very large industry that provides work for millions of people, especially actors and other performers, writers, and directors, but there are many critics who think that the economic consequences of the media have a negative effect upon the artistic. Because the potential audience for programming is so large, programmers and advertisers try to choose what will appeal to the mass. The larger the audience, the more money the TV company can charge for advertising and the more potential income the advertiser can make.

If your interest is profit, what is the point of presenting a TV series about the struggle and failure of a cancer researcher when you can present one about a beautiful actress from Montana who makes it big in New York?

On the lines below, explain why the latter program would be more desirable than the former.

_____

_____

Suppose this kind of programming decision is made by all the major programmers; describe what you think most television programming will be like:

_____

_____

In what sense is this situation desirable?

_____

_____

In what sense is this situation undesirable?

_____

_____

As you probably know, there often are great debates about the quality of television programming among the major networks. Some critics complain about excessive violence on TV shows. Others complain about immoral or amoral behavior. Still others complain about conscious or subconscious prejudice toward minority groups. And still others complain that TV has a negative influence on teachers' ability to educate youth.

What is *your* major complaint about TV programming?

___

Broadcasters argue that they carry more than just mass-appeal programs. Looking at our entire schedule, they say, the critics will see that there is something for everyone. The trouble is that critics look primarily at the programming on prime-time TV (8 P.M. to 11 P.M., Monday through Friday) when they should be examining the total schedule that runs 24 hours, broadcasters say.

State your view of the broadcasters' arguments.

___

What do you find most appealing about TV programming?

___

4. **Political:** We are using this term to mean all the ways the media affect society, affect people's thinking, and finally affect their decisions and votes.

   To many critics of the media, this is the area of deepest concern. The moment you have an audience, you have the potential for manipulation, for propaganda. When you have audiences the size we have been talking about, there are dangers. But there is also the potential for good.

Give some of your own examples of the good the media do:

___

Give some examples of how the media can be used in negative ways:

___

Give some examples of how the media actually have been used in a negative way:

Give some examples of how the media can be used in positive ways:

Before we begin our exploration of each medium individually, try to keep in mind one very important fact. If you can always remember this fact, you will have come a long way in understanding the mass media: All media are man-made. All media are forms of art, of human construction. All media are invented. No medium is objective. Every picture that you see on a TV or movie screen, or in a magazine or newspaper, every sound that comes to you via the media (TV, movies, Lp's, tapes) is the result of a careful, calculated human decision. There is nothing in the media that is natural. It appears before you as a result of human decision.

Why is this important to know? So that you do not take anything you witness in the media as the complete truth. So that you maintain your awareness that you have decisions to make, namely that there may be no truth, a little truth, or a lot of truth in what you are experiencing. You must always be aware that judgments have to be made, and you are the judge! This judging is very hard to do, but in the world of mass media, it's an obligation we have to ourselves and to a democratic society.

If men and women are making the media, we have to understand that they have motives. These motives can be perfectly acceptable: profit, instruction, entertainment, art, political change, opinion influencing. You have to be aware of these motives so that you can protect yourself from being manipulated.

The purpose of the lessons that follow is to make you aware, to help you to see and understand, and examine wisely the material you are reading right now. After all, this textbook is a medium; it's one of the media. It's a means by which you are being instructed. The author and publisher are not consciously trying to influence your opinion; rather, they are trying to help you become aware of the media and encourage you to develop your own opinions about important questions.

Throughout this text, your opinions will be requested. It is very important that you be an active participant in your own education. In order to do that, you have to be actively involved: the class needs your input, and you need to hear your own ideas, written down, expressed in speech, and shared with others. These methods are some of the key ways to develop your own ideas. To be a good ballplayer, you need to practice. To be a good thinker and an active participant in your own education, you need to practice. This textbook is going to give you a lot of practice.

Questions for Discussion and Writing

1. What are the differences between art and nature? Why, in discussing the media, is it important to know these differences?

2. Pick out one sentence or paragraph in the preceding section that you thought was interesting and describe your response to it.

3. Pick out a sentence or paragraph you disagree with and indicate the nature of your disagreement.

4. Pick out a sentence or paragraph you didn't understand completely and raise it for discussion.

5. Define the term *mass media* and give examples of it.

6. Give examples of media that are not *mass*.

7. Find and discuss at least one concrete example of mass media political propaganda. Choose from contemporary events or from history. Your school library is a good place to start your investigation.

For Further Reading

Barbour, William. *MASS MEDIA: Opposing Viewpoints*. San Diego, CA, 1994.

Bogart, Leo. *Commercial Culture: The Media System and the Public System*. NY: Oxford University Press, 1995.

Davis, Douglas. *The Five Myths of Television Power*. NY: Simon and Schuster, 1993.

Dizard, Wilson, Jr. *Old Media, New Media*. White Plains, NY: Longman, 1994.

http://www.uark.edu/depts/comminfo/www/massmedia.html

CHAPTER 2

Television: Is This Your Life?

Before we begin our discussion of television, please answer the following questions:

1. What does *television* mean? Look it up. From what language is the word derived and what do the component parts mean?

   _____

   _____

2. How many TV sets are in your home? Where are they located? Describe any special features.

   _____

   _____

3. Who watches the most TV in your house? Why?

   _____

   _____

4. Who watches the least? Why?

   _____

   _____

5. What programs do you watch every day?
   _____
   _____

6. What programs do you watch weekly?
   _____
   _____

7. What is the most popular channel in your house? Why?
   _____
   _____

8. What is the least popular? Why?
   _____
   _____

9. Estimate the number of hours the TV is on in your house every day.
   _____
   _____

10. Estimate the amount of time you watch TV every day.
    _____
    _____

11. Estimate the amount of time others in your household watch TV.
    _____
    _____

12. Using the following blank page, write an essay called (choose one):

TV in My Life	TV's Influence
What's Good About TV	How to Improve TV
What's Wrong with TV	Learning from TV
The Best Thing About TV Is . . .	Some People Have . . .Video Disease!
The Day TVs Disappeared	

Think out your essay before you start writing. Make notes about what it is you really want to say. Begin with a zinging, stabbing, sharp, or authoritative first line.

Catch the reader's attention. Establish your point, develop it carefully, and make it lively. Put some energy into your conclusion; give it some punch.

Essay _____

> • **After you have finished the essay**, let's go on. Now that you're thinking about the subject of television, let's explore it a little.

There are great controversies raging about TV and they all involve you! Programmers think about you. Writers think about you. Advertisers think about you. Commercial makers think about you. A great deal of money is spent trying to attract your attention, so, in a sense, you have a certain amount of influence. Have you ever thought about it that way? Programmers and advertisers want your attention, your opinion, your support, your vote, and your money. All of this effort to attract makes you a fairly important person.

There are other groups of people who think about you. These are TV critics and evaluators—educators, scholars, politicians, religious leaders. These people are concerned about TV's impact on your thinking, your values, morals, and ethics, and on your behavior. They are concerned that no technology has been able to dominate American life as completely and quickly as TV has. In only one generation, studies show, TV has come to occupy more of our time than any other activity except working and sleeping.

What is your opinion of this fact? Are you surprised? Does it concern you? If it does, tell why. If it does not concern you, tell why.

_____

_____

_____

_____

_____

_____

_____

_____

_____

_____

Let's see if the studies fit your case. You can participate in an experiment by keeping a strict record of your TV habits for one week, as well as the habits of your family. Keep the following charts and a pen or pencil near your favorite chair. Record (1) the TV programs you watch, and (2) the length, time, and date of each event. Do the same for an adult member of your family. At the end of the week, bring in the information you have recorded and share it with your class.

16   *You and the Mass Media*

Your record:

Program	Length	Date and Time

Totals:

Family member's record:

Program	Length	Date and Time

Totals:

> • After completing the chart, what would you say you have discovered? To what extent is it true that TV occupies more of your time than any other activity except working and sleeping? To what extent is this true of your family's habits? Enter your conclusions here.

_____
_____
_____
_____
_____
_____
_____
_____

Now let's move a little deeper into our discussion about the great debate over TV.

Consider the following remarks about television. These will give you an idea about the range of opinions that exists.

1. "The information industries of the West seemed poised to sweep away whole cultures with a vast electronic broom. Fear of American power and fear of excessive media influence went together."

    Anthony Smith,
    Director, British Film Institute

2. "TV, far from expanding consciousness, repudiates it in favor of the dream."

    Edmund Carpenter,
    Anthropologist

3. "Television is the church of modern authority. Consider, for example, the TV broadcasts of the 1953 British coronation, the funeral of John F. Kennedy, the funeral of Winston Churchill, or the marriage of Prince Charles and Lady Diana Spencer. These are the sacred occasions of modern secular culture. . . . (I)t becomes possible to see that television is worshiping state power and insisting that we do so as well."

    Michael Ignatieff,
    author of The Needs of Strangers

Chapter 2: Television: Is This Your Life? 19

4. "All television is educational television. The question is: What is it teaching?"

Nicholas Johnson,
former member of the Federal Communications Commission

5. "... I know that when someone works all day with his hands as my father did, he comes home and uses the TV set as a paintbrush to paint over the horrors of the day, to forget what real life is. I am giving people a happy pill in the nicest sense of the word."

Aaron Spelling,
producer of Charlie's Angels, Mod Squad, Fantasy Island

6. "Television is not reformable ... it must be gotten rid of totally if society is to return to something like sane and democratic functioning."

Jerry Mander,
author of Four Arguments for the Elimination of Television

7. "What Americans want from television is the dream-like and formulaic fantasies that will vent mental pressures."

Jib Fowles,
author of Television Viewers Vs. Media Snobs

8. "Television is the flickering blue parent occupying more of the waking hours of American children than any other single influence—including both parents and schools."

Kenneth Keniston,
Psychologist

9. "Their biggest enemy, many teachers say, is never present in the classroom.... It is the television set in the pupil's home."

Kate Moody,
author of Growing Up on Television

10. "I don't think the effects of television can be validly defined purely on the basis of anecdotal reports. I would feel, as a researcher, that this simply underlines the need for empirical research findings to document either alleged socially desirable or socially undesirable effects of television."

Philip A. Harding,
Office for Social Research, CBS

Although you could find 50 more quotations that are just as provocative as these, let's stop at 10. Read each one carefully and then explain each one to your kid brother or sister in terms he or she (or someone much younger than you are) will understand. Write that explanation in the space provided. Remember! Do not use the author's words; use your own!

1. _____

_____

2.

3.

4.

5.

6.

7.

8. _____

9. _____

10. _____

Divide the 10 remarks into three groups. Which ones seem to be pro-TV? Which ones seem anti-TV? Are there any that seem to you to be neutral? List the authors' names in the slots:

Pro-TV	Anti-TV	Neutral

Which quote do you agree with most?
Author _____

Which quote do you disagree with most?
Author _____

Which quote makes you think about things you may not have considered before?

Author _____

Which quote do you think is dead wrong?

Author _____

Which quote irritates you the most?

Author _____

Which quote would you like to hear more about?

Author _____

It's time now for you to do some reading on the subject of television. You're probably beginning to suspect that it is a vast field, and so it is. Because no one knows for sure the effects of television on society and individuals, or on ideas and institutions, many books and articles have been written stating strong opinions and passing serious judgment.

Following is a list of such books; your assignment is to read one of them. You'll find them in your school library or in your local public library. If your local public library doesn't have the book you want, it will be secured for you through the interlibrary loan service.

Meanwhile, examine your thoughts about one of the quotes that you have been reading. Select the one that interests you the most (or irritates, surprises, or intrigues you) and, on page 24, write an essay showing what you think of the author's ideas. In this case, you should support, reject, or qualify the author's ideas, as you see fit.

Your essay should have a strong, attractive opening in which you state your viewpoint in an interesting way. The body of your essay must develop the argument you want to present, using specific examples and explanations. Your conclusion should be firm and to the point. Be persuasive; try to have an effect on your readers and listeners.

Below is a bibliography and a Web site from which you can select your book. Of course, if you can locate another appropriate book from another source, use it.

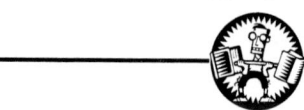

Barnouw, Erik, *Tube of Plenty: The Evolution of American Television*, 2nd Edition. NY: Oxford University Press, 1990.

Bianculli, David. *Teleliteracy: Taking Television Seriously*. NY: Continuum Publishing, 1992.

Fowles, Jib. *Why Viewers Watch: A Reappraisal of Television's Effects*. Newberry Park, CA: Sage Publications, 1992.

Gilder, George. *Life After Television: The Coming Transformation of Media and American Life*. NY: W.W. Norton, 1990.

Hirsch, Alan. *Talking Heads: Television's Political Talk Shows and Pundits*. NY: St. Martin's Press, 1991.

Kellner, Douglas. *Television and the Crisis of Democracy*. Boulder, CO: Westview Press, 1990.

http://www.uark.edu/depts/comminfo/www/massmedia.html

As soon as you get the book you want, read it quickly, taking notes. Your best bet is to put your notes on 3 × 5 cards; write only one main idea on each card so that you can arrange these notes any way you want. You want each card to function independently. On the first card, you must write down all essential information about the book: title, author, publisher, date of publication. On all subsequent cards, write the page number beneath any direct quote you take from the book.

What should you have when you have finished reading the book? You should have a stack of 3 × 5 cards that state the main points of the book and the main views of the author. Remember, each card must carry one idea only so that you can shuffle the order of the cards any way you want when you sit down to write your book report.

You should be able to see that using cards for note-taking works better than using your notebook for note-taking. You can't reassemble ideas written in your notebook easily, but you can if the notes are on cards.

Now you're ready to plan your paper.

On page 25, describe the book accurately and in detail, and indicate whether you agree or disagree with, support, or wish to challenge the author's point of view. You also want to interest the reader (the teacher, probably) and your classmates in what you've read, thought about, and written. You also want them to recall positively what you've written.

1. Create a good opening: a strong opinion or a strong quote are two possibilities. If you like the book, be persuasive in presenting it.

2. The body of your paper should describe your book precisely and in detail. Here's where your note cards come in handy. As for your opinions, you may reserve them until the end, or give them as you describe the main points. Clearly, the body of your paper must be the longest.

3. Create a strong conclusion in which you sum up what the book has to say and your view of it.

No, you're not done. This is your first draft.

(continued on page 26)

Title: _____ **Author:** _____

Read over the whole paper now, making corrections and additions and deletions. Note the style of your paper. Does it flow? Is it choppy? Does it jump around? Do you need more information? Less opinion? Let someone read your draft: a parent, a classmate, a friend. Listen to their reactions. Try to profit from those reactions by making your paper better.

After all this, now you're ready to write your final copy. Use the ruled page (page 26) that follows.

> - **After your book report has been written** and handed in, let's continue with the great debate about television. By now you should have a pretty good idea of what all the hollering is about. Because television is viewed as the most powerful of the mass media, it worries many people (we'll call them the critics) who think it degrades culture and corrupts morals. The latest statistics indicate that the average household has the TV on for a little over seven hours a day. These figures have moved steadily upward over the years. Despite the warnings of critics, people are watching television in greater and greater numbers for more hours of the day.

If you are a broadcaster (e.g., CBS, NBC, ABC, CNN), you are happy about this because you can charge more money for advertising space if you have a large audience rather than a small one.

How do you know what the size of your audience is? How can you tell an advertiser that he'll have to pay $1,000,000 for a minute of TV time rather than $500,000 or $250,000?

How would you do it? Try joining a small group of students in your class and come up with a way of finding out what Americans are watching on their TV screens at any hour of the day or night. Your method has to be fast and trustworthy, because millions of dollars of revenue are involved. Your group's job is to come up with a plan that will ensure that broadcasters and advertisers know, from one day to the next, how many Americans are watching a particular show at a particular hour. Give your plan a name. It should include the steps that must be taken.

Title: _____   **Author:** _____

The _____ Method

1. _____
2. _____
3. _____
4. _____
5. _____
6. _____
7. _____
8. _____
9. _____
10. _____

When you've concluded your original work, your teacher will explain to you the method that is actually being employed. Compare it to yours. Is yours more ingenious or less so?

_____

_____

Programming on TV is all a matter of economics. Every program is paid for by advertisers, and the amount of money advertisers pay to sell their products to millions upon millions of Americans depends on how many Americans are watching a particular program. If you are a broadcaster for NBC, you obviously want more people to watch your programs than CBS's or ABC's programs, or any of the others. It's a matter of income and profits, and a natural business sense says that you ought to stay ahead of your competition.

As a result, you watch the ratings very carefully. The ratings are a sort of counting of the votes. A low rating means you're getting a small portion of the audience to watch your program, and a high rating means you're getting a large portion of the audience. If your main job as a broadcaster is to raise your ratings (because ratings are tied to income), then you have to cancel programs with low ratings and create new programs that will get a larger portion of the audience.

TV is a big business, and to stay in business you have to be successful, which means you have to make profits. But what happens when the desire for profits conflicts with the desire for artistic excellence, social responsibility, or even, perhaps, political fairness? This is a question that bothers many people about network programming.

28 *You and the Mass Media*

Rejoin your group and list some reasons why Americans can be, and are, dissatisfied with the way programming works. See if you can find at least five reasons:

1. _____
2. _____
3. _____
4. _____
5. _____

When your group has done its task, share results with other groups and come up with a complete list of dissatisfactions. Using this list, devise changes in present American television that would create a better system. You know what's wrong with TV. Now set it right.

Here are some questions to consider as you make your changes:

1. **Programming** Study the programming for one 24-hour period. Use a copy of *TV Guide*, or remove the TV page from a newspaper. Select one network and, on the following chart, copy down its programming for a 24-hour period. Examine it carefully. Decide on a way of categorizing the programming, for instance: news shows, public affairs shows, soap operas, situation comedies, dramas, education, sport shows, movies, religious shows, children's programming, and so forth. Indicate the amount of time devoted to each category. Also make a note of when these programs appear (8–11 P.M. is considered "prime time," when most of the audience is viewing).

> - **When you have completed** categorizing the entire TV period of 24 hours, determine what should be changed in order to make television more effective, more useful, and more entertaining for the average American (including yourself, but not limited to yourself).

2. **Advertising** How would you improve the use of advertising on TV? Consider how it is presented. What would you change? Why would you change it? (Remember, you can't do away with it because without it there would be no income for the broadcasters. Without income, there would be no programming. So assume you must have advertising.) Using the chart on page 30, list 5 to 10 changes you wish to make. Give the reasons for the changes.

Category	Amount of Time	When Available

> - **After you have completed and discussed your charts** showing programming and advertising changes, conclude with a persuasive essay called "Proposals for Changes in Television." Since this will be a result of all of the reading, writing, thinking, and discussion you have done in this unit, this essay should be a substantial and convincing effort.

Begin your essay with an overview of the influence of television and the problems that grow out of that influence. Make it clear to the reader why changes are necessary and essential. (Remember, this is a persuasive essay.) The body of your essay will then present the key changes you want to see made, why you're making them, and what kind of programming you want to replace them with. Your conclusion must hammer home the need for change. Write your final copy on the ruled page immediately following the chart, though you may use more space if you need to.

Change	Reason
1.	
2.	
3.	
4.	
5.	
6.	
7.	
8.	
9.	
10.	

Proposals for Changes in Television

Chapter 3

Radio: The Intimate Medium

Unlike television, there is no great debate about radio. Critics no longer write books about the negative effects of radio on the listening audience. Lobby groups don't commit their resources to trying to pass legislation against radio's influence on the youth of America, or on the general population, for that matter. We could not put together a list of books that would be easily accessible on the problems of contemporary radio, as has been done for television in the last chapter. Why is this so?

One way to answer this question is to write an essay called "Radio in My Life" and then compare it to your observations about television, which you made in the last chapter.

So do that now, or for homework. Write the essay telling all the ways you use the radio, how much you depend upon it, how many hours a day or week you listen to it, as well as how you listen: fully? alertly? as background to other activities? Then compare and contrast it with your observations about your use of television. Use the following page for your essay.

- **After you have finished your essay,** let's talk some more about radio. We'll come back to the question why there is no great debate about radio at the end of this chapter. By then, you'll probably be able to answer the question yourself.

But first, let's take a survey of your habits:

1. How many radios do you own?

(continued on page 35)

Radio in My Life

2. How many radios are there in your house?

3. At what specific times of the day do you listen to the radio?

4. What specific stations and programs do you listen to?

5. Describe the programming of your favorite station during any specific hour of the day or night. Write down exactly what the name of the program is, who the announcer or disc jockey is, and what material is aired during the hour you have chosen. For example, what kind of news, what commercials, what songs, what messages, what kind of conversation has been transmitted?

6. Who in your family listens to the radio most? Why do you think that is the case?

7. Estimate the average number of minutes or hours a day you listen to the radio during one week.

8. Compare this number with the number you came up with for television in the last chapter. Is it larger or smaller?

9. What conclusions can you make?

When television became a new mass medium in the late 1940's and early 1950's, there were predictions from many critics and observers of the mass media that radio would soon become obsolete. Radios were going to become a relic of a former age, like the horse and carriage after the appearance of the automobile.

But this did not happen. After a short dip in popularity and a loss of revenue, radio became a thriving industry, and is reaching new heights of success today. Why do you think this is so? What needs of the audience does it serve that television does not and cannot meet?

A few moments' reflection gives us the answer: radios can go where television sets usually cannot—in your car, to the beach, in the streets, at work, in any room of your home. Radio doesn't require your immediate physical presence; it doesn't require your eyes, so you can listen while doing something else. Radio is, therefore, more flexible. Television is both a visual and auditory (listening) medium, while radio is strictly auditory. And some critics say that because sound is radio's one and only attribute, it is a great stimulant of the imagination.

All this is fairly obvious and goes a long way toward explaining why radio has been able to survive the powerful audience appeal of television.

Radio is also much cheaper to program and produce than television. After all, a radio broadcasting booth can be smaller than your kitchen, and may be staffed by one or two people at the most. Yet those two people (an engineer and announcer) can bring you news, music, messages, banter, jokes, drama, and interviews at a much lower cost than television.

The engineer and announcer need no lighting, no cameras, no costumes, no sets, no camera operators—not even makeup. Most of the time, we don't know what our favorite radio announcers look like and we don't care, because the human voice and music create a powerful enough connection for us to maintain our attention.

We said before that because sound is radio's only attribute, it is a great stimulant to the imagination. Do you agree with that statement? Or do you disagree? Contrast television and radio in this regard and explain your own point of view. Does radio stimulate your imagination more than television does? On the following ruled page, give as many reasons as you can for your point of view.

- **Now that you have finished your essay,** get ready for a real Halloween story! The most famous example of radio as a stimulant to the imagination occurred between 8 and 9 P.M. on Sunday, October 30, 1938. Have you heard of the event?

(continued on page 37 below your essay)

Essay

_____

_____
_____
_____
_____
_____
_____
_____
_____
_____
_____
_____
_____
_____
_____
_____
_____

The actor and director Orson Welles had an hour-long radio program called *The Mercury Theater of the Air*. It had been on the air for three and a half months, but CBS had to pay the show's expenses because it couldn't attract a commercial sponsor to pay the bills. Why no sponsor? Because the material was offbeat and the program was competing with a very popular show called *Charlie McCarthy* on another station. Why should a sponsor pay to advertise a product on the Welles show when it appeared the show had a very small listening audience?

On the night of October 30, 1938, Welles presented a dramatization of a science fiction novel by H.G. Wells called *The War of the Worlds*. (Was it just a coincidence that the director of the show and the novelist had the same name, with only a slight difference in spelling? One of you might volunteer to seek the answer to that question by reading one of the many biographies of Orson Welles and reporting the results to the class.)

But the dramatization didn't take place, at least not in the way you'd expect. First, there was a weather report. Then a dance band struck up some music.

Suddenly, the music was interrupted by a flash announcement that an astronomical observatory had noted a series of explosions on the planet Mars. News bulletins followed in rapid succession, interspersed with on-the-spot reports that a meteor had landed near Princeton, New Jersey. Then that report was corrected to say that it wasn't a meteor at all, but some kind of a spaceship that contained Martians armed with death rays. These Martians had come to make war upon the inhabitants of Earth!

According to Charles Jackson, a writer of radio plays and a man familiar with broadcasting techniques, he knew it was a piece of fiction from the feverish imagination of Orson Welles, so he turned the program off.

The next morning he was shocked to read and hear that people all over the United States had panicked! In New Jersey, families fled their homes. In New York, people alerted the police. Other people poured into the Princeton area to confront the invaders. In the Midwest, in San Francisco, in Pittsburgh, in Massachusetts, people were in various stages of panic. "We can only suppose," wrote Jackson, "that the special nature of radio, which is often heard in fragments, or in parts disconnected from the whole, has led to this misunderstanding."

The special nature of radio. That's a phrase we should take an interest in. What is this special nature of radio? Answer that question below with as many specific characteristics as you can come up with:

_____

_____

_____

_____

_____

As you may guess, there was a great public outcry and political clamor following the broadcast. (See pages 39–41 for newspaper accounts of the hoax.) Why do you think there was such a strong reaction? List as many reasons as you can.

_____

_____

_____

_____

_____

NEW YORK Herald Tribune

MONDAY, OCTOBER 31, 1938

Attack From Mars In Radio Play Puts Thousands In Fear

Book of H.G. Wells and Acting by Orson Welles Bring Prayers, Tears, Flight and the Police

Cry of Catastrophe Empties a Theater

Hospitals Treat Victims for Shock; Help Offered for 'Stricken' Jersey; Phone Lines Swamped

Thousand of persons in New Jersey and the metropolitan area, as well as all over the nation, were pitched into mass hysteria between 8 and 9 o'clock last night by the broadcast of a play over radio station WABC which purported to tell the story of an invasion of New Jersey, near Princeton, by inhabitants of another world. Confused reports resulting from the broadcast led to various rumors, including one that a meteor had struck near Princeton and that many persons had been killed.

The play was an adaptation of H.G. Wells' story "The War of the Worlds." It was put on by Orson Welles, twenty-three years old, actor-manager of the Mercury Theater, and had been localized in New Jersey. In Mr. Wells' story a space ship from Mars landed in Wales and the invaders began at once to lay waste to the countryside.

A Dramatic Presentation

In the Orson Welles version the space ship landed near Princeton, and its occupants at once brought weapons of fabulous power to bear on the State of New Jersey. The story was presented in highly dramatic style, with the station announcer giving the news and turning over the facilities of the station to the New Jersey "militia." A "major of the milita" gave the details of the horror in clipped sentences.

It soon became apparent on both sides of the Hudson River that thousands of persons had stumbled upon the program a little late, without knowing what they were getting into. Some tuned in just in time to get the vivid impression of a great disaster, with the National Guard taking charge and an enemy within the borders of New Jersey.

For months these same persons had subsisted upon headlines and radio broadcasts dwelling upon the imminent horrors of war in Europe, and they seemed to be in a mood to accept anything as possible. With one accord they telephoned to the nearest police station for confirmation, except for a few who didn't bother with the police, but took immediate steps for their own safety or that of their neighbors.

Mr. Welles, who had a part in the play, was amazed at its effect in casual listeners.

"There was an explosion," he said, "but it was only a small one, much like the sound of thunder. We don't believe in putting too much emphasis on sound effects, as they interfere with the action and tend to become disturbing. People who tuned in late must actually have believed that the earth was being bombarded by Martians."

A Theater Is Emptied

In New Jersey a man burst into a motion-picture theater to warn the spectators, who rose and fled. Others, in the vicinity of the Oranges, gathered their families into automobiles, threw in a few blankets and raced for the fastnesses of the Orange Mountains. One apartment house was deserted by its occupants.

It was not only New Jersey that was panic-stricken by the lurid "news" coming from the radio. Residents of North Carolina, Rhode Island, Massachusetts, Minnesota, Georgia and Alabama wept and prayed for New Jersey, fervently expressing the hope that it was not the end of the world.

The reaction to the broadcast was not always terror-stricken. Numerous physicians and nurses called up authorities in New Jersey communities offering their services in the emergency they supposed to exist.

At St. Michael's Hospital in Newark fifteen persons were brought in to be treated for shock as a result of the broadcast. The parents of six children rushed to the hospital where the children were patients, and were insistent on their immediate discharge that they might be taken to a safer part of the world.

Half a dozen women, one of them carrying a hastily packed bundle and others with children clinging to them, went to the West Forty-seventh Street police station to ask where they might find safety.

In Harlem several listeners ran to the streets in a panic, shouting that they had heard the President's voice warning them to "pack up and go north—the machines are coming from Mars." Thirty [people] raced to the West 123d Street police station and more than a dozen to the West 135th Street police station.

Telephones Are Swamped

The police of scores of communities and the newspapers too were swamped with telephone calls. At New York Police Headquarters it was estimated that more than 2,000 calls came in within fifteen minutes.

Newark police headquarters had about the same number. The Maplewood police headquarters in New Jersey, which has four switchboards, had 1,500 calls.

About a thousand calls were received at Bronx Police Headquarters. It was said that the calls were more numerous than at the time of the hurricane. At Brooklyn headquarters about three hundred calls were received.

(continued)

Mars Invasion In Radio Skit Terrifies U.S.

The police for miles around were not only overwhelmed with telephone calls, but thoroughly bewildered. Learning that the broadcast had come from WABC, they called the Columbia Broadcasting System, but the office of that corporation was itself inundated with calls and it was fifteen minutes before the police got a wire in.

In the mean time, they had queried newspaper reporters, who had called their offices, and reference to the radio programs printed yesterday morning seemed to indicate that New Jersey probably was being bombarded and destroyed only by the Wells-Welles combination. The following message was sent from headquarters to all stations and radio cars at 9:15 p.m.:

"Station WABC informs us that the broadcast just completed was a dramatization of a play. No cause for alarm."

State Police headquarters in Trenton, N.J., sent out a teletype message to the same effect.

In New York several police stations were besieged by women about whom terrified children clustered. They wanted to know what was going on and where they should go for safety.

A motorist who was parked near the Lodi Theater, a small motion-picture house on Washington Street, Orange, N.J., was lazily searching for a radio program when he was electrified by the announcement that the Columbia station was turning its facilities over to the commander of the National Guard. The voice of the "officer" followed. The motorist listened breathlessly for a moment, casting an incredulous eye meantime on the peaceful Sabbath evening street scene before him.

Then he leaped from his car and rushed into the Lodi Theater.

"The state is being invaded," he yelled, whereupon the audience leaped to its feet and made for the doors. Within two minutes the place was vacated.

Almost at once the word of impending catastrophe spread through the community and excited throngs headed for the police station. Before the crowd there became dense, however, the message from State Police Headquarters had arrived and the reassuring message was sent out that the invasion was purely imaginary.

One man who came with his family to Police Headquarters in East Orange to find out where they might seek refuge was hard to convince. For some minutes he argued with police that the whole state was in imminent danger, saying that he had "heard the President himself" say so.

While residents of the further parts of New Jersey were fleeing in panic, many of those in the neighborhood of Princeton were eager only to find the meteor, or whatever it might be which was thought to have fallen near there.

Princeton Geologists Busy

The broadcast named Grovers Mill, near the Wilson farm, as the point of impact, and long before 9 o'clock the roads leading there were jammed with cars. So great was the congestion that none could proceed and the wildest rumors flew back and forth along the line.

Professor Arthur F. Buddington, chairman of the Geology department of Princeton University, and Professor Harry Hess, mineralogist, set out with flashlights and geologists' hammers to get samples of the meteor. The parents of a dozen Princeton students sent them messages ordering them to start for home at once.

"Hell has broken out!" cried one hysterical woman who telephoned the university trying to reach her son. "It's hot even where I am."

"The Daily Princetonian" dispatched reporters after getting a telephone message from a former member of the board, now living in Montclair, who said he had heard the swish of the celestial visitor and had checked with the police, who told him that a meteor had fallen.

Two or three motorists who had radios in their cars passed through Irvington, N.J., calling to every one to drive back into the country—that the state was being bombed.

In a dozen or more communities priests telephoned the police to ask why people were hurrying into the churches in the evening.

Rahway, N.J., was one of the few communities blessed with a policeman who had read the radio program for the evening. He was Lieutenant Edwin Paine and as soon as the telephone calls began to come in, he explained that the broadcast was merely a play.

Several youths went to the Linden police station, saying that their families were exceedingly upset and wanted to know where they could find safety.

Police and fire headquarters in Trenton put on extra switchboard operators and answered more than 300 calls in an hour.

Crowd at Bar Galvanized

The East Orange police already were suffering from the plague of telephone calls when two New York motorists came bursting in. They were on their way home, they said, heading for the Pulaski Skyway, when they heard by radio broadcast that the skyway had been blown up. If there wasn't any way of getting back to the safety of New York, they said, they were going to turn around and head for the Orange Mountains. They departed without saying which way they were going. Their wives and children were in their cars, they said, and they had no time to waste.

Another telephoned that he had loaded all his family in his automobile and was ready to start. What he wanted to find out was what place would be safe.

An excited resident of Caldwell, N.J., ran into the first Baptist Church there during the evening services, shouting that a meteor had fallen, laying waste the country and that all northern New Jersey was threatened. The Rev. Thomas Thomas, pastor of the church, managed to quiet the clamor and called upon the congregation to pray for deliverance, which was done.

One of the rumors current in Newark was that there had been a severe gas explosion in the Clinton Hills district. The police sent squad cars and ambulances to Heddon Terrace and Hawthorne Avenue. They found householders on the sidewalk there with their more valuable belongings hastily bundled up beside them, ready to flee to the hills. They told the police they had heard that the district was to be subjected to a gas bombing within a short time. It required persuasive argument to get them to return to their homes.

A distracted man sought information from the Jersey City police as to where he could buy a gas mask on Sunday.

The entire country was affected by the fate of New Jersey. Women in hysterical tears besieged the switchboard of "The Providence Journal," Providence, R.I., begging for news of the dis-
(continued)

Mars Invasion In Radio Skit Terrifies U.S.

aster in New Jersey. A woman in Boston telephoned to a newspaper there that she could see the reflection of the flames in the sky. She and her neighbors, she said, were "getting out."

Plead for Disaster Details

Residents of Fayetteville, N.C., some of whom said they had relatives in New Jersey, went to the police station there with tears streaming down their faces pleading for details of the disaster. The police in Minneapolis and St. Paul were deluged with telephone calls. Anxiety was expressed by some residents of Atlanta, who thought the end of the world was at hand.

The Kansas City bureau of The Associated Press received inquiries from Los Angeles, Salt Lake City, Beaumont, Tex., and St. Joseph, Mo., as to the holocaust in New Jersey. In Birmingham, Ala., people in the street fell on their knees in prayer. A man living in Tulsa, Okla., telephoned to the radio station to see if he had time to pack his belongings before taking flight.

In San Francisco, among the hundreds who telephoned the police for information about the invasion of New Jersey was one man who wanted to volunteer at once to fight the Martians.

"Where can I volunteer my services?" he said. "We've got to stop this awful thing."

At Brevard College in North Carolina it was reported that the campus was in a panic as students fought for a chance to use telephones to ask their parents to come and get them. Five students fainted, it was said.

"The War of the Worlds" was H.G. Wells's fourth book and was published in 1898. The Welles version of it was laid in 1939 and it was said that several times during the presentation the warning was given that it was just a play.

The action was swift and fragmentary, however, and those who happened to tune in at the dramatic moments did not wait for explanations. An interlude which purported to be the broadcasting of a hotel orchestra was interrupted with the announcement that "Intercontinental Radio News Service" reported severe shocks recorded by seismographs.

People who happened to get announcements of that kind at the first turn of the dial did not wait for the happy ending planned by Mr. Welles, in which all the ferocious interplanetary invaders succumbed to the germ of the common cold.

Statement by C.B.S

The Columbia Broadcasting System issued the following statement at 11:30 p.m.:

" 'The Weekly Mercury' Theater of the Air program presented over the Columbia network tonight was an hour-long dramatization of H.G. Wells's novel, 'The War of the Worlds.' This familiar work, typical of Wells's imaginative gift, tells the story of invasion of the earth by inhabitants of Mars. The adaptation followed the original closely, but to make the imaginary details more interesting to American listeners, the adapter, Orson Welles, substituted an American locale of the English scenes of the story.

"It was announced at the beginning of the program, twice during the unfolding, and again at the end, that the program was a dramatization of an old novel. Further, the program had been scheduled so far in advance that it was publicized in newspaper listings for the hour.

"Nevertheless, the program apparently was produced with such vividness that some listeners who may have heard only fragments thought the broadcast was fact, not fiction. Hundreds of telephone calls reaching C.B.S. stations, city authorities, newspaper offices and police headquarters in various cities testified to the mistaken belief. Naturally, it was neither Columbia's nor the Mercury Theater's intention to mislead any one and when it became evident that a part of the audience had been disturbed by the performance five announcements were read over the network later in the evening to reassure those listeners."

What do you know about the rules and regulations that govern the use of the national airwaves? That govern television and radio? What do you know of the FCC (the Federal Communications Commission)? If it is little or nothing, go to the library and find out. Following your research, complete a written report on your own or make an oral report to the class.

In the Welles case, the FCC discussed taking disciplinary action, but for unknown reasons allowed the matter to pass. What do you think the FCC would do if a radio or television broadcaster tried a similar stunt today?

Suppose you are a radio broadcaster and programmer with an inventive mind and you want to try something different on your radio program? Suppose you want to startle your audience, to get their attention, which, as Charles Jackson pointed out, is hard to do because people pay only fragmentary attention to radio?

You now have the assignment to come up with an idea for a program that is as provocative as Orson Welles's. (Actually, just for the record, *The War of the Worlds* was not Welles's idea alone. It was the result of collaboration of a number of people. So don't be afraid to consult others as you work out your ideas.)

Invent a ruse or prank equal to *The War of the Worlds*. Adapt a story you are familiar with, or come up with a totally original idea that will grab the audience's attention. Don't use an invasion from outer space. Some other ideas might be the disappearance of a whole city; the discovery of a new land mass on Earth; the discovery of a new kind of human being; the sudden flowering of all plants and trees in the winter; the disappearance of all the members of your favorite football, baseball, hockey, or soccer team; the discovery of a miniature or gigantic breed of a common animal; and so forth. It's got to be something shocking.

Once you have the idea, write the script for a radio broadcast. Make it as real as possible. Include natural sound, on-the-spot interviews, interruption of normal programming, etc. On the following ruled page write it by yourself or in collaboration with others. When it is completed, present it to the class for enjoyment and evaluation.

Some Follow-up Activities

1. Bertolt Brecht (1898–1956), the great German playwright, ballad-maker, and poet, wrote a poem called "To a Portable Radio." He wrote it while he was a refugee on the run from Nazi Germany.

To a Portable Radio
by Bertolt Brecht
You little box, held to me when escaping So that your valves should not break, Carried from house to ship, from ship to train, So that my enemies might go on talking to me Near my bed, to my pain, The last thing at night, the first thing in the morning, Of their victories and of my cares, Promise me not to go silent all of a sudden.

After you read and examine the poem, answer the following:

   a. Write a paraphrase of the poem, so it is clear you know what he is saying and suggesting.

   _____
   _____
   _____
   _____

(continued on page 44)

Title: _____

b. Why is the radio so important to Brecht?

_____

_____

c. Why is radio important to you?

_____

_____

2. Write or call your local radio station. Try to arrange a visit to the studio so you can observe a radio station in operation. Ask the people who work there what their goals and purposes are. Ask them why they are in radio. Ask them how they get a license. How does one become a broadcaster?

    What schooling or training is necessary? How and why do they select the programming that goes out to the public? How big is their audience? How do they know how big the audience is? Why does the programming change? Why do some radio stations fail? Why do others succeed? Are they programming in the public interest as the FCC requires? Would they try a prank like Orson Welles's *War of the Worlds*?

3. Get a copy of your local newspaper and compare and contrast the television listings with the radio listings. What do you observe? What conclusions do you draw from these observations?

4. Distinguish between commercial radio and noncommercial radio. Go to the library and research the history of noncommercial radio. Find out what National Public Radio is. Find out if there is a noncommercial station in your area. Write or call the station and ask the the manager to explain the purposes of noncommercial radio. Draw up a list of noncommercial programming and contrast it with commercial programming.

5. Let's return to the question at the beginning of this chapter: Why is there no great debate about radio as there is about television? Why do critics say that television is encouraging violence, but they do not say the same of radio? Why do critics say that television is destroying values and taste, but they do not say the same of radio? Why do critics say that television has a bad effect on adolescents, but they do not say the same of radio? On the ruled page that follows, provide your fullest answer in an essay called "Radio versus Television." If that title doesn't interest you, make up your own.

Title: _____

Chapter 4
Film: The Big Picture

Movies are so much a part of our lives that we have many words to describe the experience. Think about it. We have: *movies, show, flick, video, cinema, film*. Can you add any others?

These words mean the same thing, but they have different connotations. That is, they may be defined the same way, but they have a different feeling from one another; they have different associations in our minds. For instance, a *movie*, a *show*, and a *flick* suggest informality. You see these with your friends and just settle back and enjoy them. *Cinema* and *film* suggest an experience that is somewhat more formal. You may belong to a film society or a cinema club. This suggests that you are taking movies more seriously; you are studying them, examining them, talking about them in a structured, purposeful way. You generally just enjoy flicks, shows, and movies, but going to the cinema is a more serious undertaking.

It seems, then, that we need more than one word because we use film in different ways. Some of those ways are entertainment, instruction, reflection, and analysis.

What is the primary way you use movies? entertainment? study? analysis? pleasure?

_____

Have you ever used movies any other way?

_____

Do you know anyone who uses film a different way than you do? Who? Why?

_____

_____

Name three movies you've seen recently.

_____

_____

Name three of your all-time favorite movies; that is, movies you've seen over and over again and continue to enjoy.

_____

_____

Why do your lists differ? What's missing in the films you named first that are present in your all-time favorite movies? Or, to put it in a more positive way, list reasons why the three you've chosen are your favorite films.

_____

_____

_____

These exercises will begin to help you formulate and verbalize concrete reasons for your taste in films. But why bother to do this? you may ask.

You read in the introduction that all media are forms of art; they are, therefore, the results of human planning, of careful, calculated human decision. Nothing in the media is natural, unlike the tree that grows outside your window.

This is most important to be aware of because all human beings have motives for what they do; trees do not have motives. A human being's motive may be to entertain, or to instruct, or to manipulate, to take advantage of your uncertainty or your weakness. It is, therefore, everyone's responsibility to watch the media alertly, rather than passively. Each individual has to be the judge of the meaning and value of the media. Nobody can make that judgment for you.

Can you think of anything you have seen in the movies that tries to influence and manipulate you? List them below.

_____

_____

Why do these efforts exist? What motives are at work?

_____

_____

This study of film will focus on analysis, reflection, evaluation, and manipulation, rather than entertainment. After all, the word *entertainment* has a kind of passive feeling to it. The dictionary says that the verb *to entertain* means *to give pleasure, to divert, to amuse*. There is nothing wrong with these activities, but they probably aren't enough to engage all of our many capacities and abilities. Do you agree or disagree? Below, give your views about (1) entertainment and (2) evaluation and analysis.

_____
_____
_____
_____
_____
_____
_____
_____
_____
_____

Now let's look at some other aspects. While diversion is a useful experience at times, many educators and critics believe that the media should be paid greater attention. They must be observed and examined. And they must be evaluated. In a democracy, each citizen should be all three things: an examiner, an observer, and an evaluator. To a small degree, we all are. We use these skills every day in our practical lives. But we often suspend our judgments. This suspension has its rewards because we can't be thinking critically every minute of the day. There are times when we just want to sit back and relax.

But suppose a movie you are relaxing through invites you, in a subtle way, to participate in some kind of antisocial behavior? With your defenses down, you might succumb to some unacceptable action.

For example, suppose a film suggests that it might be all right to commit a crime in certain circumstances. When the movie *Death Wish* was released, many people accused it of saying that being a *vigilante* (look it up if you don't know it) is acceptable if the law doesn't do a good enough job of catching criminals. Can you think of some arguments for both sides of this issue? (Who decides what is "good enough"? Does the citizen have a responsibility to fight crime?) Do you think that people could be persuaded to break the law because of something they see in a film? Can you think of other films that seem to carry a similar message? Is it the media's responsibility to warn viewers about possible consequences of viewing, or does final judgment rest with the viewer?

The suggestive power of movies is not all negative, by any means, but even in a lighthearted example, you can see the powerful effect of this mass medium on the public.

The story is told that one 1934 movie changed the underwear-wearing habits of millions of Americans. In a film called *It Happened One Night*, Clark Gable took off his shirt and lo and behold, he was naked from the waist up! He wasn't wearing an undershirt. That scene led to imitation. Men began copying Clark Gable's style with some negative consequences in the underwear industry. Do you know of any group of Americans who have copied styles they saw in movies? Clothing styles? Hair styles? Makeup styles? Shoe styles?

_____

_____

_____

Now, of course, copying a clothing style generally doesn't promote dangerous behavior. But suppose a film suggested that you honor authority no matter how cruelly the authority figure behaves? Suppose films repeat the same theme over and over, and to the exclusion of other themes? Does the issue of impact and influence, not to say manipulation, begin to loom more seriously?

In 1933 in Germany, Adolf Hitler decided to establish a Ministry for "popular enlightenment and propaganda." Joseph Goebbels, his propaganda minister, said that every film, regardless of its subject, would have a political purpose. The purpose was to control the individual and make him or her obedient to the government.

Lenin, the founder of Communism in the former Soviet Union, believed that film was the most important of all the arts. And of one film in particular, Sergei Eisenstein's *Battleship Potemkin*, Goebbels said, "This is a film which could turn anyone with no firm ideological convictions into a Bolshevik," meaning of course, a Communist.

Clearly, then, movies can and do have strong influences on people. They can make us remove our underwear, or change our political beliefs! If this is so, it then seems reasonable to say that audiences should be aware of the techniques that filmmakers employ to get the effects they want onto the screen. If viewers are always aware that what they see on the screen is a series of techniques for getting and keeping their attention, then viewers are armed and ready to deal with the media. If viewers are aware that *nothing on the screen is real except the reel it's on*, then they have come a long way toward maintaining their autonomy and judgment against the powerful forces of the media.

See if you can explain the remark italicized above to yourself. Without using the word *real* or *reel*, put that statement in your own words. Explain it to yourself.

_____

_____

All films are artistic efforts for a preconceived effect. They employ cameras, lighting, music, sound, dialogue, editing, motifs. If you consider the camera work alone, you will notice that many effects can be employed that cannot be employed in "reality." Some of those powerful effects are: close-ups, long shots, medium shots, low-angled shots, high-angled shots, tilted shots.

All of these shots are the result of choices made by talented men and women who are trying to produce a desired effect on your mind. Whether their motives are commercial or political, the techniques are the same.

Here is a list describing some of these techniques. After you read it, plan to watch a movie—any movie—and observe how and why these techniques are employed by a particular director. It would be even more advantageous if you watched a series of movies with your class and were able to evaluate the films together.

Let's start at the beginning. Movies generally start with credits. Credits are listings of all the people who have contributed to the film: the producer, director, writer, cameraperson, composer, arranger, assistant director, actors, costume designers, set designers, artists, special-effects people, casting director, continuity person, makeup people, hairdressers, and so forth. It is clear from all of this information that movies are a collaborative effort, unlike the writing of a novel, which is a very individual effort.

This army of people needs a general, and the general in a moviemaking enterprise is the director. Once a movie is funded (the producer's job), the director takes over and the success or failure of the film falls on his or her shoulders. This is why the director's name always appears last on the credits.

So from now on, when you watch a movie, take note of the credits. Take a look at all the jobs that are performed behind the camera. The so-called magic of the movies is not magic at all. The movies are the results of hard work performed by scores of skillful people led by one person, the director.

Sometimes the screen is blank behind the credits and sometimes there is action, which is called the credit sequence.

1. What is the director's name?

   _____

2. Who wrote the screenplay?

   _____

3. Who composed the music?

   _____

4. Who is the main cameraperson?

   _____

5. Who is/are the producer(s)?

   _____

6. Who is/are the editor(s)?

   _____

7. If there are special effects, who is responsible for them?

   _____

The establishing shot follows the director's name. This shot may be a very important one because some directors want the first shot to be symbolic of the film's mood. Others use the shot to establish the locale of the film, or to establish the time of the film, or a motif of the film.

Describe the opening of your film. How are the credits presented? If there is a credit sequence, describe it.

_____

_____

_____

What is the establishing shot (or sequence)? Describe it fully.

_____

_____

_____

The central and most powerful characteristics of film are photography, camera work, and editing. This is so obvious that viewers often overlook them. There are a variety of shots the camera can make: long shots, medium shots, and close-ups.

The medium shot is the most common one. If we use the human figure as a measure, in a medium shot people will be seen at full-length. They are clearly recognizable. Most of the action in a film occurs in medium shots, through which the plot develops. The close-up and long shot are used for emphasis and emotional impact. When characters enter a room, we usually see them do so in medium shots.

When the director wants to show a reaction to what's seen when entering the room, for example, he or she will select a close-up shot.

The close-up is defined as a shot of a character from the chest up. When the face fills the screen, we have a complete close-up, and when lips, or eyes, or an eyeball fills the screen, we have an extreme close-up. For the viewer, the close-up shot is the heart of the movies, because in those shots you can best understand the emotions and reactions of characters; you can feel their feelings. Without the close-up, movies would become an art without an audience.

The long shot is also used for emphasis and emotional impact. Just as the viewer wants to see the intimate reactions of the characters, he or she also wants to see the big picture, to get the general locale and perspective of the scene. (A film full of close-ups and few medium and long shots will seem claustrophobic.) The long shot sets the stage, so to speak.

On location, a long shot is a shot of a complete vista: a valley, a mountain range, a desert, a moor, a city, a city street. Long shots are useful for crowd scenes, battle scenes, scenes in which characters are running. Long shots can also be employed in a limited area, like a house. If you want to show a character's isolation, or strangeness, or mystery, long shots can be employed by using hallways, doorways, stairs.

Describe three long shots in the film you're watching.

_____
_____
_____

Describe three medium shots.

_____
_____
_____

Describe three close-ups.

_____
_____
_____

What percentage of your film contains medium shots? (Guesstimate.)

_____

What percentage of your film contains close-ups?

_____

What percentage of your film contains long shots?

_____

Angled shots of the camera can be very effective emotionally. There are high shots and low shots. There are also tilted shots. They each have their place in a film.

If the director wants a character to look larger-than-life, heroic, or strong, or if he or she wants to overpower the audience with the character's strength and confidence, then he or she will shoot upward from the ground with the sun or a mountain or a tree in the background.

If the director wants to make a character look small and insignificant, then he or she will shoot down from a height. In this manner, the character will look overwhelmed, closed-in, weak, and helpless.

If the director wants to suggest that all is wrong and awry, that sanity is being tested, then he can use a tilt shot by simply tilting the camera.

1. Describe three high shots in your film.

   _____
   _____
   _____

2. Describe three low shots in your film.

   _____
   _____
   _____

3. Describe three tilted shots, if there are any. (These are rarer.)

   _____
   _____
   _____

The camera is mobile as well. It can pan, dolly, or track; it can be handheld; it can zoom in and out.

A pan is a shot that moves slowly from right to left or left to right.

A dolly or tracking shot occurs when the camera moves along with the action or enters a stationary space.

A handheld camera can pan, dolly, or track, but gives a greater sense of intimacy, of being there. The shot jumps around because the camera is being held by a person rather than being solidly supported on a tripod or other platform.

For quick shock effects, the zoom lens is used.

1. Describe a panning shot in your film.

   _____
   _____

2. Describe a dolly or tracking shot.

   _____

   _____

3. Describe a handheld camera shot, if there is one.

   _____

   _____

4. Describe a zoom shot, if there is one.

   _____

   _____

It's important to realize that every shot in a film has a specific emotional effect. Every shot has a specific intensity. Since the medium shot is the least intense, it is the most often used. The accompanying long shots and close-ups act as intensifiers. A good director selects shots for specific reasons. He or she is aware of the emotional effects he or she wants and uses the camera to get them.

The editing of shots is another powerful way to orchestrate emotional effects. In fact, some directors say that the art of film is the art of editing; that is, after all the shooting has stopped, after all the personnel connected to the film have gone to other assignments, the art of film, these directors say, occurs in the editing room where the editor and the director decide upon the kind and sequence of shots that will make up the film. Following are the various ways to connect one scene with another. Once again, the choice of editing technique depends on the emotional effect desired.

Cut: This is the most common type of transition used within scenes and between scenes and sequences. Since a cut is a rapid action, the feeling connected to it is matter-of-fact, objective, cold.

Fade out/in: This transition is often used to indicate the passage of time. The scene fades away to darkness and the new scene emerges. Emotionally, it marks the end of one episode and the beginning of a new one.

Dissolve: A gradual transition in which the end of one scene is superimposed on the beginning of a new one. Dissolves can be long or short. Emotionally, a dissolve suggests warmth and involvement, softness.

Superimposition: The old and the new scenes are on the screen together. Compared to the three above, the superimposition is a special transition. It can be used to suggest memory, lingering thoughts, dreams, sometimes a disturbed mind. Emotionally, there is a softness and a longing in superimposition.

Jump cut: Shots are put together in such a way that there is little continuity, giving a feeling of strife, violent action, confusion.

Wipe: A shot appears to wipe the preceding one from the screen. It can move right to left, left to right, up, or down. Wipes have a light, sometimes comic effect. They are rarely used, except in comedies.

Iris: The shot becomes a circle, or an eye. The eye shuts by way of a circular movement. Or opens. This device is rare today. It also has a light, sometimes comic effect.

Freeze frame: A single shot that remains on the screen, unmoving.

In the movie you are watching for class, find examples of all of these editing devices. On the chart, indicate which are used often. Which are seldom used? Which of them are not used?

Editing Device	Used Often	Used Seldom	Not Used
Cut			
Fade out/in			
Dissolve			
Superimposition			
Jump cut			
Wipe			
Iris			
Freeze frame			

Now let's consider some other important aspects of film. Lighting is an important element in photography. The kind of lighting used in a film can have a strong psychological impact on the viewer. If brilliant light is contrasted with black shadows, the viewer feels the contrast strongly. This kind of lighting contributes to the mood of a mystery, a horror film, or a film about good and evil. A film full of grays suggests a blander, more relative mood.

Describe the kind of lighting used in your film. What mood does it suggest? Is it in keeping with the subject matter of the film? Does it fail to enhance the film? Are there sequences when the lighting works well and others when it doesn't?

_____
_____
_____

_____
_____
_____
_____
_____
_____
_____
_____
_____

Consider music. Music is a powerful factor in film-making. Because it has direct access to our feelings, it is often used as an accompaniment to the action. Music intensifies our feelings. One way to understand the power of music in a film is to turn off the sound track in a crucial scene. You will find that the emotional impact of this scene declines considerably.

Some films employ music from beginning to end. Other films use it sparingly. A few films use no music at all. Here, again, the director must decide how music or the absence of it will help his or her film.

Describe the use of music in your film.

1. Where and when does music appear in your film? When is it omitted?

_____
_____

2. Is the director's use and choice of music successful? Is its omission a wise decision?

_____
_____

Motifs are patterns that directors consciously put into their films to flesh out main ideas, themes, and moods. Motifs can be visual or auditory. You can identify them because they are repeated again and again.

Are there any visual motifs in your film? Describe them.

_____
_____

Are there any auditory motifs in your film? Describe them.

___

Just as the establishing shot introduces the movie, so the concluding shot ends it. This shot allows the director to do a number of things: display a mood, repeat a motif, round out the drama with a satisfying shot, answer a question the plot has brought to your attention. He or she does this in a visual way.

Describe the concluding shot of your film. What effect does it have? Is it a good one or a weak one? Try to guess why this particular shot was used.

___

This chapter has tried to show you the distinctive features of all films. It has isolated the different elements so that you can think about them independently. Of course, when you are watching a movie, all of these elements are interacting at the same time. From now on, it is your responsibility to do two things at the movies: (1) sit back and enjoy the totality of the film, and (2) at the same time, be aware of all the elements the director has used to make a unified film. If the film is only an average or poor one, you should be able now to determine and identify the shortcomings of the film. Now you are a critic because you can specify just why a film did or didn't work.

On the following pages, write a series of three reviews of three different movies. It doesn't matter what the movies are; it doesn't matter whether you see them on TV, in movie houses, or on videotape. What does matter is your ability to isolate and discuss the elements of film beyond the plot and the actors. Obviously, plot and characters are what interest the average untutored filmgoer. But you are no longer untutored. You are now a critic. You have skills you can employ. You have information. You know that a film is not reality no matter how real and gripping it looks. It is a work of art. It is the invention of creative men and women. It may be great, it may be poor, it may be average, it may be good. Only you can determine its value. No matter what any promoter says to the contrary, only you are the judge.

Your grades will not be given on the basis of how you rate the movies (good, poor, average, great), but on your ability to explain the reasons for the director's success or lack thereof.

Title of Movie: _____

Title of Movie: _____

Title of Movie: _____

Chapter 5

Journalism: The Great Debate

Nobody seems happy, pleased, or even satisfied with American journalism (television, radio, newspapers, magazines, and the Internet). The president isn't. Senators and members of Congress aren't. Business executives aren't. The people in the street aren't. President Nixon wasn't. Nor was President Truman. Even Thomas Jefferson, the great defender of freedom and liberty, wasn't. Are you?

You may be saying, "Who am I, compared to those mentioned?" Well, you are a potential buyer and user of television news, radio news, newspapers, news magazines, and news on the World Wide Web. You may also decide not to use, buy, or read these products. If you do, and many other people think like you, serious problems may arise that are economic, professional, and civic.

So, your opinion is important.

Are you satisfied with American journalism? Does what you see and hear on television news, on news radio, in newspapers, in news magazines, and on the Web

a. generally satisfy your need for news
b. generally dissatisfy you
c. no opinion

Circle one of the responses, and then make a statement explaining your response.

_____
_____
_____
_____

What have influential people said about American journalism in the past? What do they say today? Here is a sample: Read and discuss each one carefully.

1. "Indeed the abuses of the freedom of the press here have been carried to a length never before known or borne by any civilized nation."

    Thomas Jefferson

2. "Perhaps an editor might begin a reformation [of the press] in some way as this. Divide his paper into four chapters, heading the first *Truths*. Second, *Probabilities*. Third, *Possibilities*. Fourth, *Lies*. The first chapter would be very short."

    Thomas Jefferson

3. "I deplore . . . the putrid state into which our newspapers have passed, and the malignity, the vulgarity, and mendacious spirit of those who write them. . . . These ordures are rapidly depraving the public taste. . . . It is however an evil for which there is no remedy, our liberty depends on the freedom of the press, and that cannot be limited without being lost."

    Thomas Jefferson

4. "The history of the press is everywhere the same. In its infancy it is timid, distrustful, and dependent on truth for success. As it acquires confidence with force, it propagates just opinions with energy, scattering errors and repelling falsehood, until it prevails; then abuses rush in, confounding principles, truths, and all else that is estimable, until it becomes a serious matter of doubt whether a community derives most good or evil from the institution."

    James Fenimore Cooper, novelist

5. "I really look with commiseration over the great body of my fellow citizens who, reading newspapers, live and die in the belief that they have known something of what has been passing in the world of their time."

    Harry Truman, quoting Jefferson

6. "I don't hold with high falutin' talk . . . I'm a newspaperman. I tell stories."

    Derek Jameson, former editor, Daily Express *(London)*

7. "People may expect too much of journalism. Not only do they expect it to be entertaining, they expect it to be true."

    Lewis H. Lapham, editor

8. "The first casualty when war comes is truth."

    Senator Hiram Johnson

9. "It is the thesis here that if this balance should tip too far in the direction of the press, our capacity for effective government will be seriously and dangerously weakened."

Senator Daniel Patrick Moynihan

10. "The real source of the media's monopoly is the formidable power of repetition, totally reserved for them."

Leopold Tyrmand, journalist

11. "There is an old saying that no man can be a hero to his valet since the valet's duties make him see his employer at his most undignified. The news business now seeks the intimacy of the valet. The media peer at us from all angles and at all hours of the day and night; they love to record all our human frailties."

Walter B. Wriston, banker

12. "Who will watch the watchers?"

old proverb

13. "I have been misrepresented in the press many times."

Milton J. Schapp, former Governor of Pennsylvania

14. "I do not seek to intimidate the press, the networks, or anyone else from speaking out. But the time for blind acceptance of their opinions is past. And the time for naive belief in their neutrality is gone."

Former Vice President Spiro Agnew

15. "I have never heard or seen such outrageous, vicious, distorted reporting in 27 years of public life."

Richard M. Nixon

Well! How are you to answer these statements and charges? For you must answer them. Maybe they're all true! What then? How do you justify a free press if you can't dispute these charges? If a press can do so much damage, why shouldn't it be controlled? Who or what allows the press to be free in this country? How free is it compared with the Chinese press, the German press, the British press, the African press, the press in South America?

We think you should hold off answering these important questions for a while and first do the following survey. Find out exactly what you and your family's habits are in regard to use of the press, which represents an important part of American freedoms.

1. How many newspapers come into your home every day?

---

2. Who reads them?

3. Do you read them?

4. Why? Why not?

5. How many magazines come into your home weekly?

6. Monthly?

7. Who reads them?

8. Do you?

9. Why? Why not?

10. How much TV news comes into your home on a daily basis?

11. Who watches and listens to it?

12. Do you?

13. Why? Why not?

14. Does anyone in your home listen to news on the radio? Who listens to it?

15. Do you?
    _____

16. Why? Why not?
    _____
    _____

17. Do you have access to the Internet?
    _____

18. Do you ever look for news on the Internet?
    _____

19. Why? Why not?
    _____
    _____

Summarize your personal use of journalism news. Give your opinion, your views, your feelings, your judgments. Are you satisfied with your use, knowledge, and awareness of the news media? Why? Why not?

_____
_____
_____
_____
_____
_____

Suppose you woke up one day and there was no news . . . no newspapers, no magazines, no TV news, no radio news, no Internet. Would you miss them? Why? Why not?

_____
_____
_____
_____
_____
_____

If you were responsible for creating a brand-new society from the bottom up, what role would you give to news media? How much or how little freedom would you give?

_____

_____

_____

_____

_____

_____

We keep using the word *news*, but can you define it? Just what is *news*? What do you think it is? Consult with a classmate and, without looking at a dictionary, come up with your own definition of *news*. Write it here.

Once you've written your definition, read the definitions that follow, all of which have been written by professionals in the field:

1. "What is news? It is the honest and unbiased and complete accounts of events of interest and concern to the public."
2. "News is not what happened. It's what someone says has happened."
3. "News is not what some journalists think, but what sources say."
4. "News is not reality, but a sampling of the portrayal of reality by sources."
5. "News is an artful accomplishment which constructs social reality."
6. "News is an institutional method of making information available to consumers."

According to these suggestions, is the news ever true? There is one definition that says that. Pick it out. Then, in your own words, explain what the other definitions suggest.

_____

_____

_____

_____

_____

66 You and the Mass Media

As you can see, we have quite a disagreement about the very basic premise of journalism—the collection of news. And yet it is this very activity of journalism that helps determine the direction of political life.

Isn't this a disturbing state of affairs? Doesn't this problem make you feel a little uneasy? It should. There are journalists who call news a form of fiction. A few pages back you read that Derek Jameson, former editor of the London *Daily Express*, said, "I'm a newspaperman. I tell stories." Stories, we know, are fictional, so Mr. Jameson knows he is suggesting that journalism isn't necessarily true! Then maybe all the critics we quoted earlier are right and we ought to shut the press down! After all, if it can't tell the truth, what good is it?

Answer that question below: If journalism can't tell the truth, what good is it? Give your view and opinion. After all, what good is hearing or reading the news if it isn't the truth?

_____

_____

_____

_____

_____

In the 15 quotes given to you at the beginning of this chapter, there is a fine and satisfactory answer to these troubling questions. Can you find it? You may find it and then not agree with it. That's perfectly okay. See if you can locate it anyway. Write it below. We'll come back to it later.

_____

_____

_____

_____

Now let's go back 200 years to the creation of the Bill of Rights. The First Amendment to the Constitution of the United States forbids the government from making any laws "abridging freedom of the press." This was a completely radical idea at the time. Other governments simply assumed the right to stop any publication that they judged to be damaging to the nation. But the U.S. Constitution-makers thought differently. One of them said he would rather have newspapers without a government than a government without newspapers. This statement was made by one of the 15 writers quoted at the beginning of the chapter. Can you guess who it was? Write the name of your guess below.

_____

Examine this statement, discuss it in class, and explain its implications.

_____

_____

_____

_____

Why is freedom of the press so important if journalists themselves cannot agree upon a definition of the news and have their doubts about how to get the truth into the news? This is an absolutely crucial question. Freedom of the press is one of the great selling points of American democracy.

Whenever we look around the world and see a repressive government, one that is shutting down newspapers and other media because negative opinions about the government are flowing from them, we always say, "There! You see? That government is not democratic, the people are not free to express their views." The implication is that Americans and other people who have freedom of the press are freer, nobler, better informed, and more able to create change in society because of the existence of a free press. These are fine sentiments; these are beautiful sentiments; but if one can say that news is really the manipulation of events that occur, that news is essentially storytelling and fiction, that news is a construction of reality, not reality itself, the powerful phrase *freedom of the press* begins to wobble a bit.

Are you able to put a strong foundation under the phrase *freedom of the press*? No one can do it for you. You have to do it for yourself. Or find out you are unable to do it.

Therefore, the big task ahead of you is to examine the issue of freedom of the press in detail and to write a justification of it, or a denial of it. Why is freedom of the press a worthy belief? Or, why is it not a worthy belief? There are, after all, many countries in this world that function effectively without freedom of the press. By *function effectively*, we mean that their citizens are safe; they have ample food; they have their families, friends, and neighbors; they have jobs; they get an education. Some of these countries are quite prosperous. But they don't have freedom of the press.

Another task of yours is to find out, by using the library, what relatively prosperous countries do not have freedom of the press. What do they have in place of freedom of the press?

Listed at the end of the chapter is a short bibliography of books and Web sites you can use for your research on these important questions. Since freedom of the press is a crucial issue in our society, there is a rich supply of material on the subject. But all of these books and articles do not matter unless *you* can form a sound, defensible opinion of your own, pro or con. And that is what this chapter is all about.

Journalism is a subject of great debate in a democratic country, because some people feel the press has too much power and takes advantage of its constitutional rights. Others feel the press does not exercise enough of its rights because it is controlled by conservative forces. And there are those who say that freedom of the press is guaranteed only to those who own one! (That is, a newspaper!)

The 15 critics at the beginning of this chapter are just a very tiny sample of negative views about the press in this country. To keep a proper balance, this chapter will close with a selection of 15 positive views of freedom of the press:

1. Congress shall make no law respecting an establishment of religion, or prohibiting the free exercise thereof, or abridging the freedom of speech, or of the press; or the right of the people peaceably to assemble, and to petition the government for a redress of grievances.

    Bill of Rights, 1791, Article I (the First Amendment)

2. "In this great American democracy, we shall find that the censorial power is in the people over the Government and not in the Government over the people."

    James Madison, 1794

3. "It is time enough for government to step in to regulate people when they *do* something, not when they *say* something; and I do not believe myself that there is *any* halfway ground if you enforce the protections of the First Amendment."

    Hugo Black, Supreme Court Justice (20th century)

4. "The First Amendment is couched in absolute terms—freedom of speech shall not be abridged. . . . Free speech, free press, free exercise of religion are placed separate and apart; they are above and beyond the police power . . ."

    William O. Douglas, Supreme Court Justice (20th century)

5. "I do not admit that it is the business of this assembly to decide whether I shall or shall not publish a newspaper in this city . . . I know I am but one and you are many. My strength would avail but little against you all. You can crush me if you will; but I shall die at my post, for I cannot and will not forsake it . . . "

    *Reverend Elijah Lovejoy, publisher
    of* The Observer, *an antislavery religious journal
    in Alton, Illinois, during the Civil War era.*

6. "The press may be arrogant, tyrannical, abusive, and sensationalist, just as it may be incisive, probing, and informative. But at least in the context of prior restraints on publication, the decision of what, when, and how to publish is for editors, not judges."

    William Brennan, Supreme Court Justice (20th century)

7. "The First and Fourteenth amendments to the Constitution afford to the citizen and to the press an absolute, unconditional privilege to criticize official conduct despite the harm which may flow from excesses and abuses."

    Arthur Goldberg, Supreme Court Justice (20th century)

8. "The First Amendment requires that we protect some falsehood in order to protect speech that matters."

    Lewis Powell, Supreme Court Justice (20th century)

9. "It is well understood that the right of free speech is not absolute at all times and under all circumstances. There are certain well-defined and narrowly limited classes of speech [which are not protected]. These include the lewd and obscene, the profane, the libelous, and the insulting or "fighting" words— those which by their very utterance inflict injury or tend to incite an immediate breach of the peace."

    Frank Murphy, Supreme Court Justice, 1942

10. "A function of free speech under our system of government is to invite dispute."

    William O. Douglas, Supreme Court Justice

11. "As a Jew and a refugee from Nazi Germany, I have strong personal reasons for finding Nazis repugnant. Freedom of speech protects my right to denounce Nazis with all the vehemence I think proper. Despite my hatred of their vicious doctrine, I realize that it is in my interests to defend their right to preach it."

    Aryeh Neier, American Civil Liberties Union

12. "The Founding Fathers did not contemplate the media of radio and television when they wrote the First Amendment. [Nevertheless] their reasons for protecting the printed press from government control apply equally to the broadcast media. More people get their news from radio and television today than from any other single source. . . . If First Amendment principles are held not to apply to the broadcast media, it may well be that the constitutional guarantee of a free press is on its deathbed."

    Sam Ervin, former Senator of North Carolina

13. "It is my thesis [that] the established American press in the past ten years, and particularly in the past two years [during which Agnew and Nixon submitted their forced resignations], has performed precisely the function it was intended to perform by those who wrote the First Amendment."

    Potter Stewart, Supreme Court Justice, 1974

14. "If you want a watchdog to warn you of intruders, you must put up with a certain amount of mistaken barking. . . . But if you muzzle him

and leash him and teach him decorum, you will find that he doesn't do the job for which you got him in the first place. Some extraneous barking is the price you must pay for his services as a watchdog. A free press is the watchdog of society."

Alan Barth

15. "The best test of truth is the power of the thought to get itself accepted in the competition of the market. . . . We should be eternally vigilant against attempts to check the expression that we loathe."

Oliver Wendell Holmes, Supreme Court Justice

Discuss each of these 15 positive views in class. Which of the 15 do you agree with the most?

Why? (Explain your view.)

Which one do you disagree with most?

Why? (Explain your view.)

On the following page is a short bibliography that will help you answer the challenge we put to you to develop a sound, defensible opinion of your own, pro or con, about the value of a free press. You may want to title your essay: "Is a Free Press Essential?" You've got to be persuasive, one way or the other. Even if you take a middle ground, argue your point persuasively. You may want to quote from some of the books you have read. Most important, however, is what *you* think.

Now you can begin to address the important questions we've asked along the way, such as:

1. If a press can do damage, why shouldn't it be controlled?
2. Who or what allows the press to be free in the United States?

3. What kind of press freedoms exist in China, Great Britain, France, Italy, South Africa, Albania, Peru, Chile, Mexico?

4. One area of special interest and further research is Thomas Jefferson's mixed views of the press, for it is he who deplored and hated the press and yet wrote, "It is however an evil for which there is no remedy, our liberty depends upon the freedom of the press, and that cannot be limited without being lost." Why did Jefferson hold both views?

Use the ruled pages following the bibliography for your essay.

Bibliography

Kurtz, Howard. *Media Circus: The Trouble with America's Newspapers.* New York Times Books, 1993.

Newman, W. Russell. *Common Knowledge. News and the Construction of Political Meaning.* Chicago: University of Chicago Press, 1992.

Parenti, Michael. *Inventing Reality: The Politics of the News Media,* 2nd ed. NY: St. Martin's Press, 1993.

Sabato, Larry. *Feeding Frenzy: How Attack Journalism Has Transformed American Politics.* NY: The Free Press, 1991.

Soley, Lawrence C. *The News Shapers: The Sources Who Explain the News.*

Squires, James D. *Read All About It! The Corporate Takeover of America's Newspapers.* NY Times Books, 1993.

http://www.uark.edu/depts/comminfo/www./massmedia.html

Title: _____

CHAPTER 6

Propaganda: The Worm in the Apple

We now come to one of the most crucial problems of the mass media, and that is their influence. When we look at the term *mass media*, we see immediately why the subject is important and continually written about. Of the two words in the phrase, which one is the crucial one? If you say *mass*, most people would have to agree with you. *Media*, after all, (the plural of medium) are simply means and ways of transmission. Your artistic idea may be conveyed through the medium of paint. But is your painting a mass medium? No, unless it is reproduced in the millions.

The crucial word is *mass*, the fact that millions of people can be sent the same message at one particular moment. That immediately raises the issue of persuasion, the most important element of which is political. But persuasion, in the form of advertising, is also used in getting you to buy the breakfast food you eat. So we are talking about a wide range of areas of your life, all the way from your political freedoms to your breakfast foods.

The twentieth century has seen the greatest development of the forms of media, mass and otherwise. And at the same time we have experienced the greatest development in the use of propaganda. The books listed in the bibliography on page 80 will give you some idea of the scope and importance of this subject in this century and in world history. We're going to ask you to read and examine at least one of these books (or a similar title).

But for openers, let's ask ourselves, "What is propaganda?" Does it differ from words like:

instruction	preaching	agitation
information	indoctrination	discussion
inquiry	education	communication
persuasion	dissemination	advertising
teaching		

73

One of your goals in this chapter is to determine if there are any differences among these terms. Are they synonyms? Are they not? You are going to have to decide the answer for yourself, based on your own experiences with words, your own experiences in living, and whatever you discover in your reading and use of the mass media themselves.

The first thing to do is to go to the best dictionary you can find (your library will certainly have one) and report here the history of the word *propaganda*. How was it first used? When? By whom? Under what circumstances? From what other words is the word "propaganda" derived?

Your findings:

_____
_____
_____
_____
_____
_____

Next, provide five definitions of the word *propaganda*, from five different sources. This means you will have to consult a number of books besides the dictionary. The point of this assignment is to see whether there is general agreement over just what propaganda is. Remember to include in your definitions the connotative meaning of propaganda as well as the denotative. Both are important. We human beings attach feelings to words as well as meanings. So the word *rat* has a different feeling from the word *flower* as well as a different meaning. Feelings about words are just as important as meanings.

Your definitions (State sources):

1. _____ _____

2. _____ _____

3. _____ _____

4. _____ _____

5. _____ _____

Now go back to that list of words beginning with *instruction* on page 73. Your job is to define them and then to group them in arrangements that say, "These go together," keeping in mind the connotative meanings as well as the denotative. You must be able to defend your placement of each word in your groups. If you decide to put all the words in one group, then you'd better have a thorough defense for that decision.

Regarding the question of who'll be right and who'll be wrong in this task, you must understand that there is not always complete agreement about the connotative meaning of a word, while there may be agreement about its denotative meaning. So you may all agree about the denotative meaning of the word *preaching*, but you may have very different feelings (based on experiences) about the connotative meaning of the word.

The point, then, is not to get a right answer, but to explore how the members of your class respond to these words even after they agree on their denotative meanings. Use the ruled lines below and on the following page for your answers.

Your groups and your justifications: _____

Chapter 6: Propaganda: The Worm in the Apple   77

Next, your task is to see if you can determine, with your class, a meaning for the word *propaganda* you can all more or less agree upon. Make sure that you answer the question: Does *propaganda* have positive connotations or negative ones?

Propaganda:
_____
_____
_____
_____

Now answer the following questions:

1. Is instruction propaganda? Why? Why not?
   _____
   _____

2. Is information propaganda?
   _____

3. Is inquiry propaganda?
   _____

4. Is persuasion propaganda?
   _____

5. Is education propaganda?
   _____

6. Is advertising propaganda?
   _____

7. Is agitation propaganda?
   _____

8. Is discussion propaganda?
   _____

9. Is dissemination propaganda?
   _____

10. Is communication propaganda?
    _____

11. Is teaching propaganda?
    _____

12. Is preaching propaganda?
    _____

13. Is indoctrination propaganda?

    Can the word *propaganda* be used as a synonym for every one of the words in the list? Why? Why not?

    Is the word *propaganda* appropriate in each of the following sentences? If it is, write *yes* and explain. If it is not, write *no* and explain.

China employs propaganda.

The Nazis, governing Germany from 1933–1945, employed propaganda.

The French use propaganda.

The United States employs propaganda.

Your church employs propaganda.

Your teacher employs propaganda.

Your mother and father use propaganda in raising you.

    In your opinion, is there a difference between the phrase *the engineering of human consent* and the term *propaganda*? Explain.

    William Safire, in his *Political Dictionary* (New York: Random House, 1978), calls the word *propaganda* an "attack word"—a word that cannot be used in a neutral way. If you call something propaganda, then it is bad. Do you agree? Or do you challenge? Explain.

A term *infoganda* has surfaced in journalism. What do you think it means? What is its connotation to you?

Here are two headlines from the newspaper:

1.   EAST EUROPEAN INTEREST IN U.N. BROADENS

   Is it propaganda or a desire to make the U.N. machinery work?

2.   CHINESE FIGHT 40-YEAR-OLD PROPAGANDA WAR

Rewrite these headlines replacing the words *East European* and *Chinese* with the words *U.S.* Do you feel comfortable using the word propaganda in this new context? Would you want to change the headline around and alter a word or two? How would you do it?

Now try an exercise in propaganda. Assume that *X* no longer exists in your town or city. (*X* can be anything you think your town or city needs—more trees, more religion, more baseball, higher wages for women, an abortion clinic, cleaner air, clean politics, better relationships between citizens.) The mayor of your town or city comes to your consulting firm, of which you're president, and asks you to help him create more *X*. You agree to assist him.

You call a meeting of the mayor's staff and tell them how to persuade people to desire and obtain more *X* in their city. You show them how to use television and radio, how to employ posters. You tell them that they will have to organize parades, events, songfests. Commercials will have to be written. Prominent people, stars, celebrities will testify to the value of *X*. Something beautiful will have to be created so that people will like and want *X*.

Your first task is to determine what your *X* is. Once you (and your group, if you're working with a group) decide what it is, then:

1. Create a slogan for *X*. Keep it simple and catchy.
2. Write a commercial for the radio.
3. Write a commercial for TV.
4. Make a poster.
5. Write a lyric for a song, based on a popular tune.
6. Write the speech that will be made by the mayor at a parade.

Keep in mind that you must create something beautiful, something people will want to identify with, something appealing, something simple. Do not give them any bad news or anything with negative connotations. Keep it all simple and positive.

Before you get going, read a book about propaganda. We are providing you a short bibliography, but also check the libraries around you to see what is available on the subject. (Remember that your public library has interloan privileges and can get you a book from other libraries!) Read not only for information, but to help you solve your problem in propagandizing for *X*. Then, write a two-page outline of your plan for *X* using the ruled pages following the bibliography.

Bibliography

Chomsky, Noam. *Necessary Illusions: Thought Control in Democratic Societies*. Boston, MA: South End Press, 1989.

Herman, Edward S. *Beyond Hypocrisy: Decoding News in an Age of Propaganda*. Boston, MA: South End Press, 1992.

Lee, Martin A. *Unreliable Sources*. NY: Carol Publishing Group, 1990.

MacArthur, John R. *Second Front: Censorship and Propaganda in the Gulf War.* NY: Hill and Wang, 1992.

Pratkanis, Anthony R. *Age of Propaganda.* NY: W.H. Freeman and Co., 1992.

http://www.uark.edu/depts/comminfo/www/massmedia.html.

Music as Propaganda

> - **After finishing your plan for the mayor,** zero in on one particular type of propaganda and see what you can find out.

Can you imagine it: music as propaganda?

You say it sounds impossible, even dumb. How can music—that beautiful sound that soothes your troubles away or that makes you feel like dancing—be propaganda?

(continued on page 84)

Title: _____

84 *You and the Mass Media*

Well, think about it and recall your various experiences.

Have you ever heard someone or some group complain about music? Have you ever read a bitter denunciation of music? Can you think of at least one example in which someone has condemned a type of music? Can you think of more than one? Relate those stories and incidents below in full detail.

_____
_____
_____
_____
_____
_____

Now, explain why the music was criticized and denounced. What were the reasons given for the denunciation? Explore and explain them as fully as you can.

_____
_____
_____
_____
_____
_____

So it is possible to view music as propaganda, even though you may not feel comfortable with the idea. If the idea of music as propaganda is a new idea to you, you'll be surprised to hear that it is one of the oldest ideas in the world. People have been fearing the persuasive consequences of music since the time of the Greeks, 3,000 years ago.

The Greeks believed that music possessed something called ethos, that is, the power to influence its hearers' emotions and behavior, as well as their morals. Go to the library and read the famous myth of Orpheus to see the magic and danger of music, as it was observed in Greek mythology. Relate that story below:

_____
_____
_____
_____

The Greek philosopher Plato issued many warnings about the dangers of music. In a work called *Laws*, Plato said that the appearance of poets contributed to the breaking of musical laws, thereby causing disorder and confusion in society, which then led to a refusal to obey laws. Musical innovation, he says in *The Republic*, is the most dangerous. Change in music is the most hazardous. "For the modes of music are never disturbed without unsettling the most fundamental political and social conventions," he wrote.

Discuss the last paragraph in class, and decide for yourself whether Plato was right, and why or why not. Write your views in the space below.

Aristotle, another great Greek philosopher and a pupil of Plato, had a completely different view of music. For Aristotle, music was essentially for entertainment, relaxation, and catharsis. With it comes "a pleasant feeling of purgation and relief."

These two conflicting views of the role of music in human affairs have stayed with us up to the present day. When Christianity became the dominant force in the Western world, warnings were issued about music. While religious music was considered "good" because "a psalm forms friendships, unites those separated, and conciliates those at odds with each other," licentious songs cause passions to spring up. And at the sound of a flute, people fly into a frenzy. From there, the next step is drunkenness, and then destruction. And it all springs from the "Devil's great heap of garbage" (St. John Chrysostom, c. A.D. 345–407). Even St. Augustine (A.D. 354–430), who loved music, worried about it:

But if I am not to turn a deaf ear to music . . . I must allow it a position of some honor in my heart, and I find it difficult to assign to its proper place. For sometimes I treat it with more honor than it deserves.

—*Confessions*

Nevertheless, church music has flourished and can be viewed as an art that is designed to persuade and control. After all, music in church is expected to heighten the desired emotional effect on the listener, emphasize the text, and focus attention on the service, leaving the worshipper a stronger believer.

In the 19th century, the composers Verdi (Italy) and Wagner (Germany) used music to build national unity and dreams of superiority.

And in the 20th century, the three dictatorships of Germany, Russia, and China have taken the idea of music as propaganda very seriously. During the Cultural Revolution of 1966–1976 in China, "800,000,000 people were required to hear one of a group of eight compositions, in whole or in part, on virtually every musical or theatrical occasion. . . . Perhaps at no time in the history of music, Eastern or Western, has a society endured such an extreme censorship of the performing arts."*

Your comments are invited here:

_____

_____

_____

_____

Do we Americans use music as propaganda? That's a question you can answer by examining the very music you listen every day. Certainly the protest music of the 1960's and 1970's can be called propaganda insofar as it was antiwar, antiestablishment, pro-drug, pro-feminist, and so forth. The question for you to answer is what propaganda is being transmitted by the music of today. Join a small group of classmates and examine your CDs and tapes for propaganda. Prepare an oral report showing specifically where and what the propaganda is. Be sure you include many specific examples.

Finally, it will interest you to know that in the U.S. Army there is something called the Operations and Training Branch, Propaganda Division, Office of Psychological Warfare. One purpose of this laboratory used to be to broadcast Western music into Communist countries to compete with "the Communists' well-formulated and systematic programs of indoctrination through music." It was also the purpose of the psychological warfare to exploit the vulnerabilities of the target audience. The particular vulnerabilities were these: (1) Communist policy on music illustrates the regimes' distrust of all free and individual expression and reveals how the desire of the regimes to preserve their own power conflicts with the desires of the people; (2) A certain percentage of the audience is not satisfied by the musical

---

* Arnold Perris, *Music as Propaganda* (Westport, CT: Greenwood Press, 1985) pp. 111–112. This is a fascinating book on the subject of using music for political purposes.

diet provided by the regimes.* The goal of the Propaganda Division, then, was to use music to induce people living in Communist-ruled countries to think favorably toward Western, democratic ideas.

A final question: Is this chapter on propaganda a piece of propaganda itself? In the space below, explain why it is propaganda, or why it is not. If it is not, then explain what it is.

_____

* Nicolas Slonimsky, *Supplement to Music Since 1900* (New York: Scribner's, 1986).

CHAPTER 7

Advertising: The Big Pitch

If, as has been reported, the television set is on in the average American household for about seven hours a day, and if in every hour of network television, 15 minutes is devoted to commercials, how many hours of commercials

- do Americans see on a daily basis? _____
- on a weekly basis? _____
- on a monthly basis? _____

Let's say that in those 15 minutes of commercials per hour, 30 commercials of varied length can be run; how many commercials will the average

- American see in one day? _____
- in one week? _____
- in one month? _____

And we're just talking about television. We also have to take into consideration radio, the World Wide Web, newspapers, magazines, billboards, and advertising in the stores where we shop.

So we have to conclude that advertising is an insistent part of our lives. It's around us all the time, whether we are conscious of it or not. It this a good situation? A bad situation? How do you feel about being exposed to so much advertising?

Your response:

_____

_____

_____

_____

Now you will get involved in another great debate, and that is the debate about the justification of advertising. There are strong arguments in favor of advertising and strong ones in opposition. Read, discuss, and digest both sides with a view to forming your own considered opinion about this debate. Also, read at least one book on the subject of advertising. To that end, you will find a bibliography at the end of this chapter that will help you get started. (Don't forget that the libraries around you, both school and public, can provide you with just about any book in print, if the book you want is not available in the stacks.)

What are some of the arguments in favor of advertising?

1. Advertising calls attention to new products and to the variety of products.
2. Advertising has shortened the time for the public acceptance of new products.
3. Advertising presents information to the greatest number of people in the shortest possible time.
4. Advertising reduces the price of an item because it increases the size of the market and the number of sales.
5. Advertising increases competition and thus reduces price.
6. Advertising increases consumer confidence by making the product familiar and appealing.
7. Advertising makes the public style-conscious, thus upgrading the way people look.
8. Advertising puts millions of people to work.
9. Advertising has an educational and public service to perform, teaching the values of good health, cleanliness, etc.
10. Advertising encourages people to improve their lives.
11. Advertising increases the level of the material culture, so that yesterday's luxuries become tomorrow's necessities.
12. Packaging is individual, sanitary, and safe (compared with yesterday's bulk-buying; for example, everybody taking a pickle out of the same barrel).

That's a hefty list for you to consider. Do you like what you just read? Are there any of these 12 points that you can challenge? Indicate your immediate response on the following page.

_____

_____

_____

_____

If advertising is as beneficial as the list on the previous page suggests, why are some people opposed to it? Let's say that you are watching a fast-food commercial. You are urged to visit a restaurant and try the food, which is presented very attractively to the TV audience. You aren't warned, however, that this food is very fattening and very salty, and that if you make eating this kind of food a habit, over the years it may affect your health negatively. You may gain a lot of weight or suffer eventually from hypertension (high blood pressure). It's strictly up to you to exercise good judgment. But are you aware of the facts? Do you know the fat and salt content of the food? Do you know the possible long-range health risks? You probably don't. You are at a disadvantage against a highly professional commercial, full of humor, attractive actors, music, and visual appeal. And when you multiply this commercial by hundreds of others dealing with many other products, you begin to realize that the viewers need a great deal of information in order to make sound judgments for themselves.

What are the arguments against advertising?

> 1. Advertising exists to sell what people don't need.
> 2. Advertising is not a public service, but public exploitation.
> 3. Advertising helps to debase language.
> 4. Advertising employs muddled thinking processes.
> 5. Advertising converts raw materials of no intrinsic value into useless goods people will buy because of the pitch employed.
> 6. Advertising tells people that satisfaction can be obtained only through buying goods.
> 7. Advertising persuades people to buy a processed food that in its natural state doesn't need to be advertised.
> 8. Advertising creates needs.
> 9. Advertising creates self-doubt and anxiety.
> 10. Advertising makes people homogeneous.
> 11. Advertising makes people discontented.
> 12. Advertising induces people to be extravagant.
> 13. Advertising is antidemocratic, turning people from individuals into consumers.

Here's another hefty list for you to consider. Do you like what you just read? Are there any of these 13 points that you can challenge? Indicate your immediate response on the following page.

_____

_____

_____

_____

After you have discussed the pros and cons with your group, class, and teacher, and after you have heard various points of view, write an essay about your view of this debate. Use the two ruled pages that follow. Call it "Advertising in My Life," or "Advertising As I See It." Of course, this will be a tentative expression of your views. At the end of this chapter, you'll take another look at your developing ideas on this subject.

> - **Having written your essay** on the effects of advertising, now proceed to examine elements of advertising.

Before you sell anything, you have to know whom you're selling to. Whom are you aiming your product at? How do these people think and behave? What can you expect of them? What selling techniques will work best—that is, sell the most products? What will guarantee a *No Sale*?

Applied psychology comes in handy here. In answering these questions, advertisers have made effective use of psychology. They have come up with a series of principles regarding human behavior, which are the basis of selling techniques. These techniques are directed at you, so as you examine these principles, remember that you are the focus of them!

All human beings have needs. The key ones are to:

- eat
- hunt
- acquire
- collect
- possess
- escape from pain and suffering
- avoid disgusting objects
- be doing something all the time
- encounter emotional excitement
- be hearing, seeing, smelling, tasting, feeling all the time
- sustain a certain amount of mental activity
- overcome interference

(continued on page 94)

Title: _____

Another group of needs are social. To:

- be with others
- watch others
- be noticed by others
- show approval or disapproval
- dominate others
- be submissive and follow the leader
- love another individual
- love children

Bring a magazine to class and examine each ad in the magazine to determine which needs are being met in the ads. Can you find an ad in your magazine that does not reflect one or more of these needs?

_____
_____
_____

As a result of these needs, advertisers think that they are familiar with human motives. In other words, they know what makes you tick. They know how to appeal to you so that you will buy their products. They have listed the relative strength of particular human motives on a scale of zero to 10. Here is that list:

Motive	Rating	Motive	Rating
Appetite/Hunger	9.2	Respect for deity	7.1
Love of offspring	9.1	Sympathy for others	7.0
Health	9.0	Protection of others	7.0
Sex attraction	8.9	Domesticity	7.0
Parental affection	8.9	Social distinction	7.0
Ambition	8.6	Devotion to others	6.8
Pleasure	8.6	Hospitality	6.6
Bodily comfort	8.4	Warmth	6.5
Possession	8.4	Imitation	6.5
Approval by others	8.0	Courtesy	6.5
Gregariousness	7.9	Play/Sport	6.5
Taste	7.8	Managing others	6.4
Personal appearance	7.8	Coolness	6.2
Safety	7.8	Fear/Caution	6.2
Cleanliness	7.7	Physical activity	6.0
Rest/Sleep	7.7	Manipulation	6.0
Home comfort	7.5	Construction	6.0
Economy	7.5	Style	5.8
Curiosity	7.5	Humor	5.8
Efficiency	7.3	Amusement	5.8
Competition	7.3	Shyness	4.2
Cooperation	7.1	Teasing	2.6

Examine this list carefully. Do you agree with it? Do you think it's accurate? Do any motives seem out of place?

_____
_____
_____

What can we conclude from this list? It seems clear that self-interest is the key to people. We want satisfactions, benefits, and advantages. We want to take care of ourselves first. Others come later, except for love of offspring. Do you like this picture of human beings? Of yourself? Do you think it's true or accurate? Why might you disagree with it?

_____
_____
_____
_____

Another way of looking at the psychology of selling is this list of what people will do and won't do:

What People Will Do
People: 1. follow habit until it hurts.   2. accept their beliefs ready-made and stick to them.   3. follow leaders, eyes shut, mouth open.   4. stand by friends.   5. yield to suggestion when properly flattered.   6. look for emotional "kicks."   7. love low prices and dislike saving, holding back, economizing.   8. glorify the past and discount the future.

How does this list strike you? Write your reactions to it.

_____
_____
_____
_____

What People Won't Do
People: 1. won't look far beyond self-interest.   2. resent change; dislike the new.   3. forget the past; remember inaccurately.   4. won't fight for things when they can fight against them.   5. dare not differ from the crowd, unless the difference means superiority.   6. won't exert themselves beyond the line of least resistance, except in high emotion.   7. won't act, even in important matters, unless properly followed up.

How does this list strike you?

_____

_____

_____

_____

From all of this information and much more not provided here, advertisers come to the conclusion that:

> 1. People love themselves, are absorbed in themselves. You come first to yourself.
> 2. People are emotional. Emotions grip them deeply.
> 3. People are gregarious. They go with the crowd. They conform.
> 4. People are not practical. They don't generally reason.
> 5. People do things on whim. They don't think about the future; they think of now.
> 6. *You* is the most important word in advertising. All advertising must be written from the reader's or viewer's point of view because people want to be appealed to as individuals.

Do you find these points compelling and convincing? What are your reactions? Write them here.

_____

_____

_____

_____

The advertisers now harness these motives and principles and apply them to the products they represent. And thus we get *the big pitch* that goes on and on in our lives. We probably get to see more of *the big pitch* in the course of our lives than we do our friends or loved ones. But we try not to notice, or we don't seem to notice, which leads to an interesting problem: No one seems to know the real or actual effect of advertising on the audience. When you consider the amount of money spent on advertising (almost $60 billion in 1995), you'd think ads had some certain results. But according to studies, only 60 percent of adults remain in the room with the TV on during a commercial break and most of them read, eat, talk, and do household chores. Only about 9 percent can name the brand they saw advertised on TV immediately before answering a question about the product. A copywriter at a large ad agency was quoted as saying (anonymously, of course):

98 You and the Mass Media

Ads don't sell products, do they? Take Charlie the Tuna. Do you really go into the store and buy Starkist because Charlie the Tuna said they're picky about what they put in the can? The kind of ad that sells . . . is retail advertising, the one that says, Starkist Tuna, 15 cents off.*

Why, then, does advertising thrive? This is an important question for you to answer. After all, all of our media are paid for by advertising. All commercial TV, radio, all newspapers and magazines draw their income almost exclusively from advertising.

To pursue the point about how advertisers harness motives and principles, select 10 ads from any popular magazine and examine the techniques that have been employed to attract you to the ad.

For each one, describe what basic human motive it appeals to. Are there any other motives it appeals to at the same time? How does the ad come at you? Examine color, photography, language, point of view.

Ad #1:	
Product	**Human Motive(s):**

How will your life be better if you use this product?
_____
_____

Do you believe this ad? _____

---

* Michael Schudson, *Advertising, the Uneasy Persuasion* (New York, Basic Books, 1984), pp. 14–15.

Ad #2:	
Product	Human Motive(s):
	_____
	_____
	_____
	_____

☼ How will your life be better if you use this product?
_____
_____

Do you believe this ad? _____

Ad #3:	
Product	Human Motive(s):
	_____
	_____
	_____
	_____

✯ How will your life be better if you use this product?
_____
_____

Do you believe this ad? _____

Ad #4:	
Product	Human Motive(s):
	_____
	_____
	_____
	_____

100   You and the Mass Media

How will your life be better if you use this product?
_____
_____

Do you believe this ad? _____

Ad #5:	
Product	**Human Motive(s):**
_____	_____
	_____
	_____
	_____

How will your life be better if you use this product?
_____
_____

Do you believe this ad? _____

Ad #6:	
Product	**Human Motive(s):**
_____	_____
	_____
	_____
	_____

How will your life be better if you use this product?
_____
_____

Do you believe this ad? _____

Chapter 7: Advertising: The Big Pitch 101

Ad #7:	
Product	Human Motive(s):

☆ How will your life be better if you use this product?
_____
_____

Do you believe this ad? _____

Ad #8:	
Product	Human Motive(s):

◎ How will your life be better if you use this product?
_____
_____

Do you believe this ad? _____

Ad #9:	
Product	Human Motive(s):

102   *You and the Mass Media*

⭐ How will your life be better if you use this product?
_____
_____

Do you believe this ad? _____

Ad #10:	
Product	**Human Motive(s):**
_____	_____
	_____
	_____
	_____

⭐ How will your life be better if you use this product?
_____
_____

Do you believe this ad? _____

Now it's time for you to create your own ad! Since you now know a lot about advertising techniques, and can find out much more by reading the books in the bibliography, your assignment is to invent a product, give it a name, a slogan, and a pitch, put all of these elements together, and present your ad to your class. It can be a radio ad (put it on tape), a magazine or newspaper ad (draw it or make a collage of it), or a TV ad (put it on videotape or draw the ideas on "storyboards"). In your presentation to the class, be sure you can justify every element of your ad as effective advertising technique!

Finally, do some reading on the subject of advertising. It's a vast field and it's got a lot of avid supporters and defenders as well as critics both savage and mild. On the following page is a bibliography for your use. Check your local libraries to see what they carry on the subject.

After you've read at least one book on the subject of advertising, write a detailed description of its contents and show how your views and opinions have changed, altered, or become slightly more sophisticated. Do this on the page following the bibliography.

Bibliography

Albion, Mark, and Farris, Paul. *The Advertising Controversy: Evidence on the Economic Effects of Advertising.* Boston, MA: Auburn House, 1981.

Arlen, Michael. *Thirty Seconds.* NY: Penguin Books, 1981.

Della Femina, Jerry. *From Those Wonderful Folks Who Gave You Pearl Harbor.* NY: Simon and Schuster, 1970.

Ewen, Stuart. *Captains of Consciousness: Advertising and the Social Roots of the Consumer Culture.* NY: McGraw-Hill, 1976.

Glatzer, Robert. *The New Advertising.* NY: Citadel Press, 1971.

Danna, Sammy R. *Advertising and Popular Culture.* Bowling Green, OH: Bowling Green State University Popular Press, 1992.

Gartner, Michael G. *Advertising and the First Amendment.* NY: Priority Press, 1989.

Key, Wilson Bryan. *The Age of Manipulation: The Con in Confidence, the Sin in Sincerity.* NY: Henry Holt, 1989.

Schudson, Michael. *Advertising, the Uneasy Persuasion.* NY: Basic Books, 1984.

Title: _____ **Author:** _____

CHAPTER 8

Censorship

> I found that to tell the truth is the hardest thing on earth, harder than fighting in a war, harder than taking part in a revolution.
>
> *Richard Wright,*
> *American novelist,*
> *short story writer, and journalist*

Let's talk about censorship.

A censor, someone or some institution that practices censorship is: (1) an official who examines publications for objectionable matter and then deletes forbidden material; (2) the psychic agency in the mind that represses unacceptable notions before they reach your consciousness.

Thus, we find ourselves in two completely different arenas: the political and the mental.

Can you think of a variety of examples of censorship, real or imagined?

Give examples of government censorship:

_____

_____

_____

Give examples of religious censorship:

_____

_____

_____

Give examples of censorship in schools:

_____
_____
_____

Give examples of censorship in your social group:

_____
_____
_____

Give examples of censorship in your home:

_____
_____
_____

Give examples of censorship in your head (self-censorship):

_____
_____
_____

We find, clearly, that there is censorship all around us, and in us. And yet we are forever describing our freedoms, demanding our freedoms, extolling our freedoms. Is this a contradiction? A paradox? A reality? How do you explain the fact that censorship is in every part of our lives and yet we praise the freedoms we have, and fight to the death if any of those freedoms are threatened?

Read and examine the four quotes that follow. Comment on each one as the spirit moves you. The purpose is to get a flow of reaction going. After reading this chapter, and the earlier ones, you should have something substantial to say about each one of these. There are no right or correct responses:

a. "In 80 percent of the countries in the world today, guys like myself would be in jail."

Art Buchwald
(Find out who he is, if you don't know.)

_____
_____

b. "No one is entitled to the truth."

E. Howard Hunt
(Find out who he is, if you don't know.)

c. "When a person goes to a country and finds the newspapers filled with nothing but good news, he can bet there are good men in jail."

Daniel P. Moynihan
(Find out who he is, if you don't know.)

d. "It is by the goodness of God that in our country we have those three unspeakably precious things: freedom of speech, freedom of conscience, and the prudence never to practice either of them."

Mark Twain
(Find out who he is, if you don't know.)

Few issues cause more controversy in human affairs than censorship. People want to know the truth, and governments are often very busy suppressing it for a variety of reasons, some of which you would probably agree with.

The issue of censorship is not a simple one because it occurs on so many levels—from the international all the way to the individual and psychological. And often, people have contradictory and paradoxical attitudes about censorship, so that citizens may denounce their governments for political censorship but censor their own children on other grounds, i.e., moral.

It seems, from all the evidence, that human beings are natural censors and, at the same time, opponents of censorship. The controversy rages on and the elemental questions should be everpresent in our minds:

> 1. Why, in the first place, do human beings censor? Why is there any censorship at all?
> 2. Why are both desires so strong in us: the desire to censor, and the desire to stop censorship?

These questions will make exciting original research projects as long as you realize that you'll be studying theories and opinions rather than facts. Nevertheless, drawing together a number of these theories and opinions into a coherent and interesting paper will go far in helping you think about censorship.

Now you're ready to write that well-thought-out, well-crafted essay on the questions posed to you at the beginning of this chapter and above. Pick the one you think you can do the best with and spend a few days on it in order to do a thorough job. Use the ruled pages that follow for your final draft.

Title _____

Keep firmly in mind that we can argue about free speech, and demand it as well, because of the First Amendment to the United States Constitution, which reads:

"Congress shall make no law respecting an establishment of religion, or prohibiting the free exercise thereof; or abridging the freedom of speech, or the press; or the right of the people peaceably to assemble, and to petition the Government for a redress of grievances."

There it is: the foundation of freedom in our democracy. You agree with it; I agree with it. Why, then, are there endless arguments, battles, and struggles about free speech in this country? Not a week passes without a controversy about freedom of speech. Here are some important questions about free speech. Read each one and then write your opinion on the lines provided.

Should there be limits on free speech? _____

_____

Should there be less violence and sex in movies and on television? _____

_____

Should there be less violent and sexual language on radio? _____

_____

Should books that insult religious groups or use vile language or describe grossly violent acts be censored?

_____

_____

Should the news media be regulated? _____

_____

Does national security justify censorship? _____

_____

Is school and library censorship justified? _____

_____

Should pornography be censored? _____

_____

Should people who preach hatred and violence be censored? _____

_____

Should people who preach the overthrow of government be censored?

_____
_____

Do teenagers have the same rights as adults? Do they have the right to debate these questions with adults? Do they have a right to help shape discussions about their moral lives?

_____
_____

Should a lockout feature be available on all TV channel-switching devices so that parents can monitor what their children see?

_____
_____

Should there be censorship on the Internet? Should software be available to parents to block parts of the Internet?

_____
_____

Every one of these questions is a hotly debated issue. You may ask why. After all, the First Amendment is crystal clear: "Congress shall make no law . . . abridging the freedom of speech, or the press. . . ." But your mother and father aren't Congress. Your school board isn't Congress. Your community isn't Congress. Your local churches and temples aren't Congress. Your own conscience isn't Congress. There are many times when these entities act as censors. Are they acting against the First Amendment? Are groups of citizens correct when they say they are defending and enforcing local standards of decency in censoring a book, a movie, a teacher? After all, Congress is far away. We all live in communities that want to be peaceful, orderly, and as free of controversy as possible. We have standards of decency we want to uphold. We want to live in communities that uphold Judeo-Christian principles. Why permit a book, a movie, a TV show, a person, a tape, a computer program to tear at that fabric just because of some abstract statement written over 200 years ago, a period of time that has little in common with our frenetic mass media world?

In the following pages, you are going to be confronted with a series of First Amendment controversies and you are going to be asked to make decisions and judgments about them. If these questions seem easy or remote, remember that you will be parents someday and you will be confronting questions in regard to *your* children's lives and values and beliefs. And if you have belief and faith in the First Amendment, you're going to sweat over these questions.

Confrontation 1: A small town library has scheduled a series of lectures on tarot card readings, astrology, numerology, and dream analysis. But a group of churchgoers objected that their tax dollars were being used to promote Satan worship and the occult. They said that these lectures would cause evil forces to enter people's lives. The library board, under pressure, canceled the lectures. The head librarian, however, comes in conflict with the board because her job is to resist all efforts at censorship of library materials and information. Meanwhile, a local resident who dabbles in tarot and astrology spreads the word of the cancellation on the Internet. Soon, defenders of the lectures, some from distant communities, are picketing the library. Controversy begins to inflame a quiet town, dividing the librarian and the library board, dividing members of the community. The churchgoers are interested in maintaining their religious standards. They think they are reflecting the majority's values. The librarian and her supporters are interested in defending the First Amendment's right to free speech. The picketers agree with the librarian.

Where do you stand on this issue? What ought to be done, according to you? Is there a way of settling this thorny issue with a compromise? Must there be winners and losers? The churchgoers are clearly censors and, under their pressure, so is the library board. But they say that they reflect the majority's values. Are they enemies of the First Amendment? Probably not, but they are saying that on these particular topics they must make an exception and force the prohibition of the lectures.

Form a group with four or five of your classmates and fully examine the issues and the possible solutions. Present them to your whole class.

Confrontation 2: A political commentator has said that the only way to have a free press in the United States is to own one. Other than that, you and I and every writer in America are subject to censorship. This is a very harsh judgment and seems to make a mockery of the First Amendment. The commentator's remark implies that, despite the First Amendment, many factors enter into decisions about censorship. They may be political, ethical, moral, and financial. And they are often local decisions, made without even thinking about the First Amendment. If I'm a newspaper owner and I have to make a decision about printing a story that may hurt my paper's circulation and income, I may discard it for obvious reasons. Why hurt myself? It's all well and good for an outsider to promote the First Amendment, but when your personal interests are at stake, it's an altogether different matter.

Take the case of Brett Easton Ellis's novel *American Psycho*. The novel was accepted, edited, and printed, and was ready to be shipped to bookstores all over the U.S. in 1990 when the publisher abruptly canceled the shipments.

What happened? The publishing house changed its mind when a powerful women's organization complained, after reading excerpts in magazines, that it was a novel attacking women in a particularly vicious way. The main character is a serial killer who dismembers women. When these stories spread in the media, the president of the parent corporation that owns the publishing house "became aware of its contents" and canceled the book a month before the shipping date. The decision was "a matter of taste," the president said. A year or so later, an abridged version of the novel was published in paperback by another publisher. No one, including the president of the corporation, had read the book in its entirety. He said only that he "became aware of its contents," and obviously canceled it because of negative publicity. No one, it seems, had read the novel in its entirety, and yet many people had strong opinions about it. And they voiced them with the results mentioned.

How do you evaluate this case? Is it an example of censorship or an example of editorial judgment? Or of a response to public pressure? Or fear of negative publicity?

Just remember that no one in the media, except the editor of the novel, had read the entire book. Critics were responding to excerpts. One writer who read the entire novel said it was "hypnotic, discomforting, amusing, apocalyptic, annoying, infuriating. . . ." He said if novels are to be more than mere entertainment, then they've got to go into some dark corners of human behavior, however unpleasant. He concluded by saying that only those who have read the book should have anything to say about it.

Nevertheless, enough people who didn't read the entire book had plenty to say about it, and distribution was canceled.

Form a group and examine the questions raised above. Draw your conclusions and present them to the class.

One of you may be curious enough to read the expurgated version of *American Psycho* that's available in Vintage paperback and report your findings to the class in a book report or an oral report.

Confrontation 3: The following statements were written in 1973 by William O. Douglas, a member of the Supreme Court of the United States at that time:

"The First Amendment was designed to invite dispute, to induce a condition of unrest, to create dissatisfaction with conditions as they are and even to stir people to anger. The First Amendment was not fashioned as a vehicle for dispensing tranquilizers to the people. Its prime function was to keep debate open to offensive as well as staid people. . . . The materials before us may be garbage. But so is much of what is said in political campaigns, in the daily press, on TV, or over the radio. By reason of the First Amendment . . . speakers and publishers have not been threatened or subdued because their thoughts and ideas may be offensive to some."

The following statements were made by Phyllis Schlafly, president of the Eagle Forum, an organization that promotes and defends traditional and family values:

> *"We can all probably agree that* Playboy *and* Hustler *should be prohibited for use in the public school classroom. Once we make that admission, it is clear that we are not wrestling with weighty issues of First Amendment or academic freedom, but merely with matters of judgment as to what is wise and appropriate to give to other people's minor children, and at what age. . . . But who gave the curriculum dictators the authority to select books that challenge the children's religion, values, or parents? How did such books get into the public schools in the first place? Don't the rest of us have any First Amendment rights not to be forced to read materials we find offensive?"*

Examine each quotation, determine its strengths and weaknesses, and decide which one you support and which you reject. Give your reasons. You may do this individually or in groups. In either case, be persuasive about your decision.

Is it possible to agree with both comments? Or disagree with both comments? If one or the other is your position, explain it fully.

Confrontation 4: After being used and praised by doctors and surgeons for 50 years, a famous German anatomy atlas has come under attack. It is suspected that the bodies used in the detailed illustrations may be those of victims of Nazi brutality and the Holocaust. It is a fact that the author, Dr. Eduard Pernkopf, was a member of the Nazi party and became dean of the Vienna medical school when Hitler invaded Austria in 1938. He and a group of artists worked on the book until his death in 1955. Early editions of the book contained artists' signatures decorated with swastikas and the letters "S.S." In postwar editions, these symbols were removed.

Some American doctors want the book banned because it was produced under evil conditions: Its author and staff were committed Nazis and supporters of Hitler, and the cadavers were victims of Hitler's murderous regime. One doctor said, "The creator was evil, and the book has no place in any medical library. I suggest that it be tossed into the waste bin of time."

On the other hand, other doctors think that Dr. Pernkopf's atlas is a masterpiece: an outstanding book—complete, thorough, and authoritative. When a new edition was reviewed in 1990, it was called a classic and the illustrations were called works of art. There is an opinion that says it doesn't matter that Dr. Pernkopf wasn't a good person and belonged to the wrong political party.

Assuming the above information to be correct, if not exhaustive, should Pernkopf's anatomy atlas be banned? Should it be replaced by another anatomy atlas of equal merit that doesn't have a depraved history? Today, some doctors say, there are computer models and CD-ROM's of high quality that could easily replace this particular controversial anatomy book. One person has suggested that a memorial page be placed at the front of the atlas, saying that many of the cadavers used for illustration were people murdered by the Nazis. Another commentator said that in any banning, two new victims would be created: our democracy and the First Amendment.

What do you say? Form a group, hammer out your point of view after considering the aspects of the debate, and present your conclusions to the class. Is it possible, by the way, that there isn't enough information to come to a definitive conclusion?

The free speech debate is endless. As long as the First Amendment exists, there will be fiery clashes among (1) those who believe that any and all expression is protected, (2) those who want what they would call "reasonable" restrictions, and (3) those who would be strict censors.

The Internet, for example, cannot escape the focus of this debate. How much free expression should be permissible on the Internet? Again, there are those who believe that prohibiting indecency on the Internet means limiting all materials in cyberspace to that which is acceptable for children. These limitations are unacceptable, they say.

Then there are those who focus on sex and violence on television, in pop music, and in the movies. Many of these people want the entertainment industries to monitor themselves by self-restriction and labeling. The industries have agreed to self-restriction because they fear that public pressure about indecent and violent content might lead to laws that would include fines and prison sentences for disobedience. Then, of course, the industries would appeal. This appeal could get to the Supreme Court, where a final decision would be made; final, that is, until the next First Amendment case comes before the nine judges.

Here are some addresses you can write to or e-mail for further information on all aspects and points of view about censorship and the First Amendment:

Accuracy in Media: 1275 K. Street NW, Washington, DC

American Booksellers Association: 137 W. 25 Street, New York, NY 10001–7296

American Civil Liberties Union: 132 W. 43 Street, New York, NY 10109–0592

American Civil Liberties Union: e-mail: ftp://pipeline.com/aclu

American Family Association: Box 2440, Tupelo, MS 38803

American Library Association: 50 East Huron Street, Chicago, IL 60611

Christian Coalition: P.O. Box 1990, Chesapeake, VA 23327

Morality in Media: 475 Riverside Drive, New York, NY 10015

National Coalition Against Censorship: 275 Seventh Avenue, New York, NY 10001

Parents for Rock and Rap: P.O. Box 53, Libertyville, IL 60048

Wired: 520 3rd Street, 4th floor, San Francisco, CA 94107–1815

Wired: e-mail: info@wired.com and www.wired.com/4.10/netizen/

A very lively article called "The Rights of Kids in the Digital Age" can be found at www.wired.com/4.07/kids/.

Now you're ready to write that well-thought-out, well-crafted essay on the questions posed to you on the previous pages. Here are some ideas, phrases, or themes that may help organize your thoughts. Pick the one you think you can do the best with and spend a few days on it in order to do a bang-up job.

1. Is it hard to tell the truth?
2. Why is it so hard to tell the truth?
3. Censorship is not just a political matter.
4. Aspects of censorship
5. Who's free? Who's not?
6. A truly free press
7. The struggle for free expression
8. The right to speak out
9. Censorship is more complex than I thought.
10. The complexity of this world
11. Is censorship in a free society desirable?
12. Should any book, movie, music be censored?
13. Should the Internet be regulated?

Title: _____

_____
_____
_____
_____
_____
_____
_____
_____
_____
_____
_____
_____